THE SOLDIER'S CATECHISM

THE SOLDIER'S CATECHISM

Virtuous Warriors in an Age of Terror

A Manual
for the Spiritual Fitness
of the US Armed Forces

MICHAEL E. CANNON, JR

Solid Ground Christian Books
Birmingham, Alabama USA

Solid Ground Christian Books
2090 Columbiana Rd, Suite 2000
Birmingham, AL 35216
205-443-0311
sgcb@charter.net
http://solid-ground-books.com

THE SOLDIER'S CATECHISM
Virtuous Warriors in an Age of Terror

Rev. Michael E. Cannon, Jr.

Solid Ground Classic Reprints

First edition February 2006

Cover work by Borgo Design, Tuscaloosa, AL
Contact them at nelbrown@comcast.net

1-59925-054-3

THE
SOLDIER'S
CATECHISM

THE SOLDIER'S CATECHISM

Composed for those serving in or allied to the United States Armed Forces

Consisting of two Parts: Wherein are chiefly taught,

1. *The Justification of our Soldiers*
2. *The Qualification of our Soldiers*

Written for the Encouragement, and Instruction of all that have taken up Arms in this Cause of God and His People; especially the common Soldiers.

By Michael E. Cannon, Jr.

First Edition

2 Samuel 10:12 *"Be of good courage, and let us be courageous for our people, and for the cities of our God, and may the LORD do what seems good to him."*

Deuteronomy 23:9 *"When you are encamped against your enemies, then you shall keep yourself from every evil thing."*

To all the valiant and faithful Soldiers that have engaged themselves in the Service of the United States and her allies for the glory of God, and advancement of liberty everywhere.

TABLE OF CONTENTS

INTRODUCTION

𝕿 he Soldier's Catechism emerged during the English Civil Wars as part of the *"New Model Army"*, the most famous of the Parliamentarian Armies. In addition to being an Army of expertly trained soldiers led by trained military commanders, the soldiers of the Cromwellian Army retained the reputation of one of the most virtuous Armies ever to take the field of battle due largely to their Puritan religious zeal. The New Model Army was stood up on February 15, 1645 from the existing "Roundhead" forces. Oliver Cromwell removed the existing leadership when he passed a *"self-denying ordinance"* and replaced it with trained leaders. The tactics of the New Model Army were based on fast hit-and-run attacks against the flanks of the enemy, a revolutionary evolution in strategy for its time. The Army was comprised of 22,000 soldiers, including 11 regiments of cavalry (6600 men), 12 regiments of infantry (14400 men), and 1 regiment of 1000 dragoons. Like our Army today, promotions were based on proficiency rather than social standing or wealth. The New Model Army's victories reflected their virtue. Often against great odds, their commitment to their cause, and their courage, steadied by their unwavering faith in God, drove them on to victory. After the end of the civil war, they fought in Scotland, Ireland, Flanders and Spain. After the campaigns in Ireland in the 1640's some of them retired to settle in what is now called Northern Ireland.

This present catechism represents the first serious attempt to bring the Soldier's Catechism current and apply it to the conflicts and Armies of the 21st Century. The questions have been modified only where necessary to make them relevant to modern times rather than to the English Civil War, i.e., references to Parliament and King have been replaced.

The Soldier's Pocket Bible and The Second Chapter of *The Westminster Confession of Faith* covering the Trinity have been added resources in the appendix. The *Pocket Bible* originated in the same historical period as the Catechism; only the biblical texts have been updated to the English Standard Version (ESV). This *Pocket Bible* was intended to provide a soldier with a conveniently sized bible for reference and encouragement in the unique context of war. (A second edition was eventually published titled "The Soldier's Penny Bible.")

Wherever possible I have sought to retain the sense of antiquity in the language when it did not detract from the modern interpretation.

Michael E. Cannon, Jr.

"God hath work to do in this world; and to desert it because of its difficulties and entanglements, is to cast off His authority. It is not enough that we be just, that we be righteous, and walk with God in holiness; but we must also serve our generation, as David did before he fell asleep. God hath a work to do; and not to help Him is to oppose Him."   John Owen, Volume IX, p. 171

"His divine power has granted to us all things that pertain to life and godliness, through the knowledge of him who called us to his own glory and excellence, [4]by which he has granted to us his precious and very great promises, so that through them you may become partakers of the divine nature, having escaped from the corruption that is in the world because of sinful desire. [5]For this very reason, make every effort to supplement your faith with virtue, and virtue with knowledge, [6]and knowledge with self-control, and self-control with steadfastness, and steadfastness with godliness, [7]and godliness with brotherly affection, and brotherly affection with love. [8]For if these qualities are yours and are increasing, they keep you from being ineffective or unfruitful in the knowledge of our Lord Jesus Christ. [9]For whoever lacks these qualities is so nearsighted that he is blind, having forgotten that he was cleansed from his former sins. [10]Therefore, brothers, be all the more diligent to make your calling and election sure, for if you practice these qualities you will never fall. [11]For in this way there will be richly provided for you an entrance into the eternal kingdom of our Lord and Savior Jesus Christ."
                                          2 Peter 1:3-11

PART I

The Justification of our Soldiers

[1]

Question: **Of what Profession are you?**
Answer: *I am a Christian and a Soldier. Christian Soldiers fight against the Flesh, the World, and the Devil; and since I call myself Christian, I fight against my own unholy desires.*
James 4:1, *"What causes quarrels and what causes fights among you? Is it not this, that your passions are at war within you?"*
1 Peter 2:11, *"Beloved, I urge you as sojourners and exiles to abstain from the passions of the flesh, which wage war against your soul"*

THOUGHTS FOR INSPIRATION:
"I had rather have a plain russet-coated captain that knows what he fights for, and loves what he knows, than that which you call a gentleman and is nothing else."   *Letter from Cromwell to Sir William Spring, Sept. 1643*

"God has brought us where we are, to consider the work we may do in the world, as well as at home."   *Oliver Cromwell to the Army Council, 1654*

"I am a soldier, I fight where I am told and I win where I fight."
General George S. Patton

"For peace is not mere absence of war, but is a virtue that springs from, a state of mind, a disposition for benevolence, confidence, and justice"   *Baruch Spinoza*

"Temperance is simply a disposition of the mind which binds the passion."
Thomas Aquinas

"From the time I was twelve years old until I retired last year at the age of fifty-seven, the Army was my life. I loved commanding soldiers and being around people who had made a serious commitment to serve their country."

General Norman Schwarzkopf

REFLECTION: TEMPERANCE

Temperance is a virtue of independence. It is the power of our rational mind to overcome our irrational (natural or emotional) impulses. A temperate man is concerned with *quality* instead of *quantity* for the sake of quantity. An intemperate man becomes so focused on acquisition and indulgence that the pleasure he once derived from the object of his desire no longer gives him pleasure in the way it once did. Food, sex, smoking, or any other pursuit becomes the master, and the man becomes the slave. Moderation in all things is better than losing ourselves to pursue all things.

STUDY AND MEDITATION: PHILIPPIANS 1:20-21

"...as it is my eager expectation and hope that I will not be at all ashamed, but that with full courage now as always Christ will be honored in my body, whether by life or by death. For to me to live is Christ, and to die is gain."

In the passage from Philippians 1, Paul has determined that his life is committed to glorifying God. He has a purpose and is so focused on it that even in death he sees it as the culmination of his service to God.

Many Christians have separated not only church and state but life and faith. Like two tracks for a train running side by side, they seem to never cross. For Paul, life and faith had merged into one purpose, a monorail system of life. Even in death, he was confident that he served the purposes of his faith which was to progress the Gospel of Christ.

Christian soldiers are not Christians and soldiers, they are one whole person that is all Christian and all soldier. Therefore, everything a soldier is and does must be consistent with everything a Christian is called upon to do and held accountable for before God. There cannot be a dual life in one person but a single-mindedness serving one God.

DOCTRINE: From the Heidelberg Catechism (1563)
Q. 32, Why are you called a Christian?

Because I am a member of Christ by faith, and thus am partaker of His anointing; that so I may confess His name, and present myself a living sacrifice of thankfulness to Him; and also that with a free and good conscience I may fight against sin and Satan in this life, and afterwards reign with Him eternally, over all creatures.

[2]

Question: **Is it lawful for Christians to be soldiers?**
Answer: *Yes, without a doubt: we have enough evidence to believe it.*
1. *God calls Himself a Man of War and the Lord of Hosts.*
   Exodus 15:3, The LORD is a man of war; the LORD is his name.
2. *Abraham had a regiment of 318 trained men.*
   Genesis 14:14, "When Abram heard that his kinsman had been taken captive, he led forth his trained men, born in his house, 318 of them, and went in pursuit as far as Dan."
3. *David was employed in fighting the Lord's Battles.*
4. *God taught David to fight*
5. *David trusted God's providence in war.*
   1 Samuel 17:45, 46, "Then David said to the Philistine, 'You come to me with a sword and with a spear and with a javelin, but I come to you in the name of the Lord of hosts, the God of the armies of Israel, whom you have defied. This day the Lord will deliver you into my hand...'"
6. *The noble gift of valor is given for this purpose.*
7. *The New Testament mentions two famous Centurions*
8. *John the Baptist did not require Soldiers to leave their professions, Luke 3:14*
9. *Many comparisons are taken from this Calling in the New Testament*
   Philippians 2:25 "I have thought it necessary to send to you Epaphroditus my brother and fellow worker and fellow soldier, and your messenger and minister to my need"
   2 Timothy 2:3-4, "Share in suffering as a good soldier of Christ Jesus. No soldier gets entangled in civilian pursuits, since his aim is to please the one who enlisted him."
10. *There have been many famous Martyrs of this Profession.*

THOUGHTS FOR INSPIRATION:
"The only thing necessary for the triumph of evil is for good men to do nothing."   *Edmund Burke*

"The hottest places in Hell are reserved for those who in time of great moral crises maintain their neutrality."   *Inscription at the Entrance to Hell;*
From The Inferno

"In the sphere of religion, as in other spheres, the things about which men are agreed are apt to be the things that are least worth holding; the really important things are the things about which men will fight."

J. Gresham Machen

CHRISTIAN MILITARY LEADERSHIP:

"While Germany struggled under the political and religious consequences of [Martin] Luther's reform movement, the movement itself quickly spilled out of the German borders into neighboring Switzerland. At the time, Switzerland was not so much a single country as a confederacy of thirteen city-states called cantons. When Luther's ideas began to pour over the border, several of the cantons broke from the Catholic church in Rome and became Protestant while other cantons remained firmly Catholic. Of the cantons that adopted Luther's new movement, the most important and powerful was the city-state of Zurich under the leadership of Ulrich Zwingli (1484-1531).

Zwingli brought to Luther's revolution an education steeped in northern Humanism, particularly that of Erasmus. He was monumentally popular in Zurich for his opposition to Swiss mercenary service in foreign wars and his attacks on indulgences; he was, in fact, as significant a player in the critique of indulgences as Luther himself.

Zwingli rose through the ranks of the Catholic church until he was appointed "People's Priest" in 1519, the most powerful ecclesiastical position in the city. However, by 1519 he had bought fully into Luther's reform program and began to steadily shift the city over to the practices of the new Protest church. In 1523, the city officially adopted Zwingli's central ecclesiastical reforms and became the first Protestant state outside of Germany. From there the Protestant revolution would sweep across the map of Switzerland."[1]

"Zwingli himself died on the battlefield, in the prime of manhood, aged forty-seven years, nine months, and eleven days, and with him his brother-in-law, his stepson, his son-in-law, and his best friends. He made no use of his weapons, but contented himself with cheering the soldiers. 'Brave men,' he said (according to Bullinger), 'fear not! Though we must suffer, our cause is good. Commend your souls to God: he can take care of us and ours. His will be done.'"

"Soon after the battle had begun, he stooped down to console a dying soldier, when a stone was hurled against his head by one of the

Waldstätters and prostrated him to the ground. Rising again, he received several other blows, and a thrust from a lance. Once more he uplifted his head, and, looking at the blood trickling from his wounds, he exclaimed: 'What matters this misfortune? They may kill the body, but they cannot kill the soul.' These were his last words."[2]

REFLECTION: RESOLUTION

A resolute man is one that is decided on his purpose. He is fixed in his determination; hence, bold; firm and steady. He has concluded his debate on a matter and focused himself on the task at hand. He has committed his resources to accomplish the mission.

STUDY AND MEDITATION: 2 TIMOTHY 2:3-4

"Share in suffering as a good soldier of Christ Jesus. No soldier gets entangled in civilian pursuits, since his aim is to please the one who enlisted him."

In 2 Timothy 2, Paul encouraged Timothy to accept the hardship that comes from serving Christ in this world. It is easy to note the suffering of those who are in service to Christ and become discouraged. The natural human tendency is to seek ease and prosperity in the present rather than serve to receive our reward in the eternal future. Paul wants Timothy to keep his courage and not shrink back when he hears of Paul's misfortune. His guidance is thus, don't get so caught up in your worldly affairs or vocations that you cannot serve Christ. Paul doesn't demand that we have no way to make a living. He simply encourages us to keep the things that are passing away in perspective and not let them overwhelm us and consume all our energy and attention to the exclusion of serving Christ. Like soldiers on the battlefield, we must engage the purposes of Christ as our first aim. Everything else in life is secondary to that.

DOCTRINE: SECOND HELVETIC CONFESSION (1566)

XXX.4, And if it be necessary to preserve the safety of the people by war, let him do it in the name of God; provided he have first sought peace by all means possible, and can save his subjects in no way but by war. And while the magistrate does these things in faith, he serves God with those works which are good, and shall receive a blessing from the Lord.

[3]

Question: **What then does our Savior mean by those words in Matthew 5:39?** *"But I say to you, do not resist the one who is evil. But if anyone slaps you on the right cheek, turn to him the other also."*
Answer: *There Christ does not only forbid private revenge and resistance, but also public wars for private ends. Scripture is the best interpreter of Scripture; and we cannot find one place of Scripture that warrants raising up an Army in civil disobedience.*

THOUGHTS FOR INSPIRATION:
"Forgiveness is the key to action and freedom."   *Arendt Hannah*

"Those who forgive most shall be most forgiven."   *Festus Bailey*

"God examines both rich and poor, not according to their lands and houses, but according to the riches of their hearts."   *Augustine of Hippo*

"There is no justice among men."   *Czar Nicholas II*

"Justice and power must be brought together, so that whatever is just may be powerful, and whatever is powerful may be just."   *Blaise Pascal*

"He that cannot forgive others breaks the bridge over which he must pass himself; for every man has need to be forgiven."   *Lord Herbert*

"Doing an injury puts you below your enemy;
Revenging one makes you but even with him;
Forgiving it sets you above him."   *Benjamin Franklin,*
POOR RICHARD'S ALMANAC

"When I say I love Eastland, it sounds preposterous—a man who brutalizes people. But you love him or you wouldn't be here. You're going to Mississippi to create social change—and you love Eastland in your desire to create conditions which will redeem his children. Loving your enemy is manifest in putting your arms not around the man but around the social situation, to take power from those who misuse it—at which point they can become human too."   *Bayard Rustin*

"Little men cannot forgive."   *Unknown*

REFLECTION: PEACEFULNESS

For a soldier, *peaceable* doesn't mean that there is always peace. A peaceable man is one who does not seek trouble. A man who has a quiet and gentle spirit that respects others and himself. A man that trusts God to care for the matters related to justice and feels no compulsion to vindicate himself in a sudden act of rage or revenge. But like a trained falcon, a peaceable man is capable of action when it is necessary. The difference between a peaceable man and a man of violence is the cause for which either one will strike another.

STUDY AND MEDITATION: MATTHEW 5:39

Matthew 5:39, "But I say to you, Do not resist the one who is evil. But if anyone slaps you on the right cheek, turn to him the other also."

In Matthew 5:39, "*Do not resist*" is often used in the context of litigation. It means that we are not to retaliate against an individual because of the evil act they do against us. Matthew 5 does not teach that we should not take action against the principle of evil in the world. Rather than a passive acceptance of evil and injustice, Jesus is teaching us not to insist on our personal rights but to surrender judgment and justice to God as He judges the hearts of men from the heavenly courts. That means this verse speak directly to personal application and principally to national and political interpretation.

DOCTRINE: WESTMINSTER CONFESSION OF FAITH (1647)

XXXIII.1, God hath appointed a day, wherein he will judge the world, in righteousness, by Jesus Christ, to whom all power and judgment is given of the Father. In which day, not only the apostate angels shall be judged, but likewise all persons that have lived upon earth shall appear before the tribunal of Christ, to give an account of their thoughts, words, and deeds; and to receive according to what they have done in the body, whether good or evil.

[4]

Question: **What side are you on? And for whom do you fight?**
Answer: *I am for the United States of America, or in plainer terms;*
1. *I am a Warrior and a member of a team. I serve the people of the United States and live the Army Values.[3]*
2. *I am a guardian of freedom and the American way of life.[4]*
3. *I fight to uphold the Laws and Liberties of my Country, which are always in danger to be overthrown by those who oppose Freedom in every age.*

4. *I fight for the preservation of our Government, in which (under God) consists the glory and welfare of the United States; if this foundation is overthrown, we shall soon be the most slavish Nation in the world.*

5. *I fight in the defense and maintenance of true faith, which is now violently opposed, and will be utterly suppressed in this world if we are not victorious against the legions that have raised up against our true religion.*

THOUGHTS FOR INSPIRATION:

"This nation will remain the land of the free only so long as it is the home of the brave."   *Elmer Davis*

"Oh, how strenuous is life! I know a little of it. Men *'ought always to pray, and not to faint.'* How fierce the battle! I know something of the conflict, but I ought not to faint, because I can pray."   *G. Campbell Morgan*

"... human will-power alone is not enough. Will-power is excellent and we should always be using it; but it is not enough. A desire to live a good life is not enough. Obviously we should all have that desire, but it will not guarantee success. So let me put it thus: Hold on to your principles of *morality* and *ethics*, use your willpower to the limit, pay great heed to every noble, uplifting desire that is in you; but realize that these things alone are not enough, that they will never bring you to the desired place. We have to realize that all our best is totally inadequate, that a spiritual battle must be fought in a spiritual manner."
            D.M. Lloyd-Jones

"We are an Army at war, and we expect to remain at war for a prolonged period. We'll be an Army at war until the job is done and every last one of them who threatened this great nation of ours are put in their place." *Gen. Kevin P. Byrnes*

REFLECTION: FIDELITY

In all the many virtues a man can possess, there are some that emerge as essential for the others to have meaning. Fidelity (or *faithfulness*) is one virtue that provides direction for all the others. Fidelity is associated first with our *memory*. For example, if we don't remember the principles that made our nation great or our own respect for the dignity of man (ontological worth), then we will have little use for the virtue of *courage* to defend those principles or the virtue of *integrity* to speak about those things we ought to remember and respect. When a man decides to be virtuous, he must learn to remember. Virtue then begins in the mind and moves to the heart and hands. Perhaps an individual must first learn what is worthy of remembering! In every case, we must have a history that gives us direction if we are to have a future.

STUDY AND MEDITATION: VARIOUS

Psalm 37:14-15, *"The wicked draw the sword and bend their bows to bring down the poor and needy, to slay those whose way is upright; their sword shall enter their own heart, and their bows shall be broken."*

Deuteronomy 1:30, *"The LORD your God who goes before you will Himself fight for you, just as he did for you in Egypt before your eyes"*

Isaiah 50:8, *"He who vindicates me is near. Who will contend with me? Let us stand up together. Who is my adversary? Let him come near to me."*

Joshua 10:25, *"And Joshua said to them, 'Do not be afraid or dismayed; be strong and courageous. For thus the LORD will do to all your enemies against whom you fight.'"*

1 Samuel 18:17, *"Only be valiant for me and fight the LORD's battles."*

Joshua 24:14-15, *"Now therefore fear the Lord and serve him in sincerity and in faithfulness. Put away the gods that your fathers served beyond the River and in Egypt, and serve the Lord. And if it is evil in your eyes to serve the Lord, choose this day whom you will serve, whether the gods your fathers served in the region beyond the river, or the gods of the Amorites in whose land you dwell. But as for me and my house, we will serve the Lord."*

Being Christian is always a deliberate act. The category of "cultural Christian" is one made and embraced by people unwilling to submit themselves to the call of discipleship. There is no allowance made for that sort of faith and life in the Scriptures. While the call of Christ to follow after Him and adhere to His teaching is clear, the siren call of the world is overwhelming and alluring. Appeals to the carnal nature can be so compelling that the most disciplined disciple might falter without the preserving power of the Holy Spirit. In many cases, accommodation and toleration have subsumed all other virtues, including fidelity. The world lures the Christian into a quiet complacency that lacks a sense of stewardship to the call of Christ. Joshua 24 makes it clear that there is no compromise allowed for the godly man or woman. Jesus reiterates his demand for fidelity in the book of Revelations when He promises to "spit out" the lukewarm. Faithfulness and commitment, even if it is to the flesh, is preferred to compromise, hypocrisy, and indifference. How can we be indifferent to the cause of Christ, to the seriousness of our call, to the coming of the Kingdom of God and the life that is eternal? It is rightly said that the opposite of love is not hate but indifference. Better to be for or against something than to simply not care. Choose this day where you stand and whom you serve.

DOCTRINE: HEIDELBERG CATECHISM

Q. 127 , *"And lead us not into temptation, but deliver us from evil"*, that is, since we are so weak in ourselves that we cannot stand a moment; and besides this, since our mortal enemies, the devil, the world, and our own flesh, cease not to assault us, do Thou therefore preserve and strengthen us by the power of Thy Holy Spirit, that we may not be overcome in this spiritual warfare, but constantly and strenuously may resist our foes till at last we obtain a complete victory.

[5]

Question: **Isn't your struggle for freedom a struggle against *all* power and authority that might be over you?**

Answer: *No not at all, yet many in this world do abuse authority and power to take freedom and liberty away from men rather than preserve and protect it. Our only object is:*

1. *To rescue our Nation from the dangers that surround it in order to maintain that liberty that God has granted us.*
2. *When power and authority are used to take life and subjugate a free people to the rule of a despot then our struggle will be against that particular power and authority.*
3. *We strive to defend that which we have promised to defend, by our oath and the trust given to us by the American people.*
4. *We take up Arms against the enemies of faith who make war against people in order to subvert religion and freedom of conscience.*
5. *If the leadership of our nation is willing to take a stand for the sake of Liberty and the American people, then certainly both we and all good citizens may lawfully stand in the defense of both, as the people did against King Saul, in 1 Samuel 14:45.*
6. *We are called upon to do no more than our forefathers when they came into this great land with a godly vision and fought for their freedom and liberty to establish America as a beacon of hope drawing all men who desire liberty to her shores. Their selfless service and courage liberated a people. They remain justified in what they did to all posterity by our faithful stewardship of the freedoms handed down to us.*
7. *We will not waste the blood of our fathers by shirking the responsibilities placed upon us by the evils of our day but we will honor their sacrifice by securing the freedoms that their blood purchased for us.*

THOUGHTS FOR INSPIRATION:

"The love of liberty is the love of others, the love of power is the love of ourselves." *William Hazlitt, 1778-1830*

"The power that is supported by force alone will have cause often to tremble." *Lajos Kossuth*

"The greatest virtues are those which are most useful to other persons." *Aristotle*

"He is no fool who gives that which he cannot keep to gain what he cannot lose." *Jim Elliot, missionary martyr*

REFLECTION: SELFLESS SERVICE
Selfless service is essentially showing unselfish concern for the welfare of others by providing assistance or help. It goes much deeper than simply being helpful in the utilitarian sense. Paid servants can be helpful. The person who cultivates selfless service as an aspect of their character will also exhibit humility and a unique ability to empathize with others. They will cultivate a vision to see others with compassion rather than competition. They will seek opportunities to help without recognition rather than responding out of necessity and expecting praise. A person with a character willing to be selfless in their service to others or in support of ideals receives their satisfaction by knowing God knows their hearts as He knows the hearts of all men and that nothing escapes his notice. Ultimately, *selfless service* is following the example of our Lord who was misunderstood even as He offered the most definitive example of selfless service for us to follow.

STUDY AND MEDITATION: ROMANS 13:1-5

"Let every person be subject to the governing authorities. For there is no authority except from God, and those that exist have been instituted by God. Therefore whoever resists the authorities resists what God has appointed, and those who resist will incur judgment. For rulers are not a terror to good conduct, but to bad. Would you have no fear of the one who is in authority? Then do what is good, and you will receive his approval, for he is God's servant for your good. But if you do wrong, be afraid, for he does not bear the sword in vain. For he is the servant of God, an avenger who carries out God's wrath on the wrongdoer. Therefore one must be in subjection, not only to avoid God's wrath but also for the sake of conscience."

While the ultimate authority in all things rests with God alone, he uses means on earth to accomplish His ends. Like a mechanic that uses a tool or an instructor that uses speech, so God chooses to use means to His ends. God created man as a social and interactive creature.

Consequently, men have always come together in communities and live together in agreement with laws and certain social virtues in an environment of mutual trust. Those laws have consistently been based upon the Word of God. When a person or a group determines to violate those laws to seek their own advantage at the expense of others, it becomes a corruption to the entire organization. God has ordered society so that man would be free to live cooperatively and be able to follow the path God has laid before him. When others seek to steal from some men that liberty to obey God, governments are commissioned to intervene. These governments that stand for truth and liberty operate as agents of God for the good of mankind. All men in all places are commanded to recognize God's commission of those governments who willingly serve the cause of God in the persecution of evil.

DOCTRINE: WESTMINSTER CONFESSION OF FAITH

XXIII.1, God, the supreme Lord and King of all the world, hath ordained civil magistrates, to be, under Him, over the people, for His own glory, and the public good; and, to this end, hath armed them with the power of the sword, for the defense and encouragement of them that are good, and for the punishment of evil doers.

[6]

Question: **Hasn't the Constitution guaranteed the maintenance of our laws, liberties, and religious freedoms? Why then do we fear the subversion of them?**
Answer:

1.   *Many things have been published for governments since time immemorial and many can be seen in historical archives. Those who wrote the documents whether for good or bad have passed from this life to the next. Paper alone cannot guarantee the perpetuation of our Republic, Freedom, or an Orderly Society.*
2.   *Though our elected representatives mean well and intend to do good, there are those that fail to understand how precious and fragile the Liberty of man can be and unintentionally subvert our freedom by their lack of prudence.*
3.   *We cannot imagine that any other nation will rise to defend the Liberty of Americans.*

4.   *There are some secular deconstructionist that will distort justice to change a government from free and representative to oppressive and authoritarian.*

THOUGHTS FOR INSPIRATION:

"I am an American, fighting in the forces which guard my county and our way of life. I am prepared to give my life in their defense."

Article I of the US Armed Forces Code of Conduct

"A man's country is not a certain area of land, of mountains, rivers, and woods, but it is a principle; and patriotism is loyalty to that principle." *George W. Curtis*

"War is an ugly thing, but not the ugliest of things. The decayed and degraded state of moral and patriotic feeling which thinks that nothing is worth war is much worse. The person who has nothing for which he is willing to fight, nothing which is more important than his own personal safety, is a miserable creature, and has no chance of being free unless made or kept so by the exertions of better men than himself."   *John Stuart Mill*

"A patriot is necessarily and invariably a lover of the people. But even this mark may sometimes deceive us. The people are a very heterogeneous and confused mass of the wealthy and the poor, the wise and the foolish, the good and the bad. Before we confer on a man, who caresses the people, the title of patriot, we must examine to what part of the people he directs his notice. It is proverbially said, that *he who dissembles his own character, may be known by that of his companions.* If the candidate of patriotism endeavors to infuse right opinions into the higher ranks, and, by their influence, to regulate the lower; if he consorts chiefly with the wise, the temperate, the regular, and the virtuous, his love of the people may be rational and honest. But if his first or principal application be to the indigent, who are always inflammable; to the weak, who are naturally suspicious; to the ignorant, who are easily misled; and to the profligate, who have no hope but from mischief and confusion; let his love of the people be no longer boasted. No man can reasonably be thought a lover of his country, for roasting an ox, or burning a boot, or attending the meeting at Mile-end, or registering his name in the lumber troop. He may, among the drunkards, be a hearty fellow, and, among sober handicraftsmen, a free-spoken gentleman; but he must have some better distinction, before he is a patriot."

Johnson: The Patriot

REFLECTION: PATRIOTISM

Patriotism is both emotional and reflective. It is a commitment to a national vision manifest in a present cause or undertaking. A love of country is a love of principle, not geography. When America was founded, being patriotic held few rewards. The penalty for patriotism was severe until the conclusion of the Revolution. Patriots see a cause beyond themselves that is worthy of their devotion. They have a passion to uphold the higher principles because they see in them a calling for all men to live a better, more virtuous life. They see in the national ideals a godliness that inspires them to follow the leadership's vision with an assurance that it is inspired and blessed by God. Patriots may be in short supply but with a clearly articulated national vision, a new generation of patriots may yet emerge from the clouds of confusion into the light of virtue, reason and faith.

STUDY AND MEDITATION: DEUTERONOMY 16:18-20

"You shall appoint judges and officers in all your towns that the LORD your God is giving you, according to your tribes, and they shall judge the people with righteous judgment. You shall not pervert justice. You shall not show partiality, and you shall not accept a bribe, for a bribe blinds the eyes of the wise and subverts the cause of the righteous. Justice, and only justice, you shall follow, that you may live and inherit the land that the LORD your God is giving you."

Benjamin Franklin wrote, *"Let all your things have their places; let each part of your business have its time."* Orderliness may not seem to be an important virtue until you consider the alternative, *chaos.* Children begin in chaos and mature into orderliness. In fact, one of the signs of maturity is the order of life: adjustments to allow for vocation, meeting schedules, and cooperating with others. For a society to move forward, there must be order in all things. When God created the earth, He brought order out of chaos. When man sinned, he brought chaos back into the ordered world he lived in. We are to strive for well ordered lives and a well ordered society.

"Just as in its religious worship the Israelites were to show themselves to be the holy nation of God, so was it in its political relations as well. Civil order—that indispensable condition of the stability and prosperity of nations and states—rests upon a conscientious maintenance of right by means of a well-ordered judicial constitution and an impartial administration of justice."[5]

DOCTRINE: WESTMINSTER CONFESSION OF FAITH

XX.1, God alone is Lord of the conscience, and hath left it free from the doctrines and commandments of men, which are, in any thing, contrary to His

Word; or beside it, in matters of faith, or worship. So that, to believe such doctrines, or to obey such commands, out of conscience, is to betray true liberty of conscience; and the requiring of an implicit faith, and an absolute and blind obedience, is to destroy liberty of conscience, and reason also.

XX.2, They who, upon pretense of Christian liberty, do practice any sin, or cherish any lust, do thereby destroy the end of Christian liberty, which is, that being delivered out of the hands of our enemies, we might serve the Lord without fear, in holiness and righteousness before him, all the days of our life.

[7]

Question: **How can you, as a Christian and a soldier, claim to be free from any authority but God and yet answer to Paul in Romans 13:1-5 where he teaches:**

"Let every person be subject to the governing authorities. For there is no authority except from God, and those that exist have been instituted by God. Therefore whoever resists the authorities resists what God has appointed, and those who resist will incur judgment. For rulers are not a terror to good conduct, but to bad. Would you have no fear of the one who is in authority? Then do what is good, and you will receive his approval, for he is God's servant for your good. But if you do wrong, be afraid, for he does not bear the sword in vain. For he is the servant of God, an avenger who carries out God's wrath on the wrongdoer. Therefore one must be in subjection, not only to avoid God's wrath but also for the sake of conscience."

Answer:

1.   *Those verses of Scripture do not require obedience to any unlawful commands, nor does any other place in Scripture. We cannot obey man any further than a command is able to stand the testing of Scripture.*

2.   *Those that say the government is the highest power are grossly mistaken. Indeed, the government and our President are the highest powers in this land and perhaps even in the world, but the Laws and the Courtrooms of this land are above him in power, and the President himself is limited and subject to the Supreme court in the land: Therefore law is higher than political power and law carries force only when it is founded in God's Word.*

3.   *Even if the President of the United States were the supreme power; if he decided to cause or even permit the destruction of our Nation, both*

natural law and the grace of God allows (in other places called First and Second causes) people to preserve themselves.

THOUGHTS FOR INSPIRIATION:

"We the people of the United States, in order to form a more perfect union, establish justice, insure domestic tranquility, provide for the common defense, promote the general welfare, and secure the blessings of liberty to ourselves and our posterity, do ordain and establish this Constitution for the United States of America."   *Preamble for the US Constitution*

"[The prosperity of the United States] is not the result of accident. It has a philosophic cause. Without the *Constitution* and the *Union*, we could not have attained the result; but even these are not the primary cause of our great prosperity. There is something back of these, entwining itself more closely about the human heart. That something, is the principle of *"Liberty to all"*— the principle that clears the *path* for all—gives hope to all—and, by consequence, *enterprise* and *industry* to all."   *Abraham Lincoln*

"The very idea of the power and the right of the People to establish Government presupposes the duty of every individual to obey the established Government."   *George Washington (Farewell Address)*

"The strength of the Constitution lies in the will of the people to defend it."
     Thomas Edison

RELECTION: SELF-CONTROL

Self-Control can sometimes be described as *self discipline*. It is the effort to subjugate impulse to reason. A self-controlled man is one that has enough will power to do what he knows is right even when he feels pulled in another direction by his base and carnal desires. Without self-control, a man will ultimately self destruct. He will excessively indulge in food, pleasure, work, or any other number of activities that are meant for good but without the control of reason, destroy.

STUDY AND MEDITATION: ROMANS 13:1-5

"Let every person be subject to the governing authorities. For there is no authority except from God, and those that exist have been instituted by God. [2]Therefore whoever resists the authorities resists what God has appointed, and those who resist will incur judgment. [3]For rulers are not a terror to good

conduct, but to bad. Would you have no fear of the one who is in authority?
Then do what is good, and you will receive his approval, ⁴for he is God's
servant for your good. But if you do wrong, be afraid, for he does not bear the
sword in vain. For he is the servant of God, an avenger who carries out God's
wrath on the wrongdoer. ⁵Therefore one must be in subjection, not only to
avoid God's wrath but also for the sake of conscience."

Christians are called to separate themselves from the passions and desires of
the fleshly world and yet, Christians find themselves still living in the world
and subject to secular authority and law. Paul insists that the Christian must
have a high regard for secular authority and submit to it as a matter of
conscience. The Christian recognizes that all of creation belongs to God and
that it is bound by natural law. God has determined to govern the world by
both natural law, i.e. gravity, aging, seasons, etc and delegated authority to
civil governments. Just as God has delegated authority to parents, employers,
elders in the church and others, He has also given authority to secular
governments to keep the civil law for the good of society and the peace of the
people. The civil authority becomes the organized center of the community
that will provide all that the people of God need for peace and survival.

DOCTRINE: WESTMINSTER LARGER CATECHISM
Q **128**. *What are the sins of inferiors against their superiors?*
A. The sins of inferiors against their superiors are, all neglect of the duties
required toward them; envying at, contempt of, and rebellion against, their
persons and places, in the lawful counsels, commands, and corrections;
cursing, mocking, and all such refractory and scandalous carriage, as proves
a shame and dishonor to them and their government.

[8]

Question: **What is it that motivates you to take up arms, and commit**
yourself in war?
Answer:
1. *The love I have for my Country*
2. *The preservation of our Republic, Laws, and Liberties*
3. *The defense of our Faith against those who desire to oppress it.*
4. *The care of our posterity*
5. *The general progress of all good people*

6.   *The command of the President of our Nation, who, under the law, is the highest elected authority in our land.*

7.   *The necessity that now lies upon all that fear God in the Land to rise up and defend all that is sacred against evil.*

THOUGHTS FOR INSPIRIATION:

"For anything worth having one must pay the price; and the price is always work, patience, love, self-sacrifice—no paper currency, no promises to pay, but the gold of real service."   *John Burroughs*

"The purpose of all war is peace."   *Saint Augustine, 354-430*

"The art of war is, in the last result, the art of keeping one's freedom of action"
                    Xenophon, Greek historian (c. 430-355 BC)
                    Flavius Vegetius Renatus (ca 390 AD)

"A nation, as a society, forms a moral person, and every member of it is personally responsible for his society."   *Thomas Jefferson*

"I have no private purpose to accomplish, no party objectives to build up, no enemies to punish—nothing to serve but my country."   *Zachary Taylor*

"Let us have the faith that right makes might, and in this faith let us to the end dare to do our duty as we understand it."   *Abraham Lincoln*

"Humility must always be the portion of any man who receives acclaim earned in the blood of his followers and the sacrifices of his friends."
                    Dwight D. Eisenhower

"The energy, the faith, the devotion which we bring to this endeavor will light our country and all who serve it, and the glow from that fire can truly light the world."   *John F. Kennedy*

"The tree of liberty must be refreshed from time to time with the blood of patriots and tyrants. ... Resistance to tyrants is obedience to God."
                    Thomas Jefferson

REFLECTION: REVERENCE
There are some things in life that have intrinsic qualities that demand and inspire our reverence. We should be in awe when we consider God. God made everything from nothing and yet he has called us his own. He has ordered the universe and yet he is patient with our struggles and difficulties. When we consider Him as He is, we should not falter in our steps when we have confidence that we are in His will.

STUDY AND MEDITATION: DEUTERONOMY 1:19-32

"Then we set out from Horeb and went through all that great and terrifying wilderness that you saw, on the way to the hill country of the Amorites, as the LORD our God commanded us. And we came to Kadesh-barnea. And I said to you, 'You have come to the hill country of the Amorites, which the LORD our God is giving us. See, the LORD your God has set the land before you. Go up, take possession, as the LORD, the God of your fathers, has told you. Do not fear or be dismayed.' Then all of you came near me and said, 'Let us send men before us, that they may explore the land for us and bring us word again of the way by which we must go up and the cities into which we shall come.' The thing seemed good to me, and I took twelve men from you, one man from each tribe. And they turned and went up into the hill country, and came to the Valley of Eshcol and spied it out. And they took in their hands some of the fruit of the land and brought it down to us, and brought us word again and said, 'It is a good land that the LORD our God is giving us.' "Yet you would not go up, but rebelled against the command of the LORD your God. And you murmured in your tents and said, 'Because the LORD hated us he has brought us out of the land of Egypt, to give us into the hand of the Amorites, to destroy us. Where are we going up? Our brothers have made our hearts melt, saying, "The people are greater and taller than we. The cities are great and fortified up to heaven. And besides, we have seen the sons of the Anakim there."' Then I said to you, 'Do not be in dread or afraid of them. The LORD your God who goes before you will himself fight for you, just as he did for you in Egypt before your eyes, and in the wilderness, where you have seen how the LORD your God carried you, as a man carries his son, all the way that you went until you came to this place.' Yet in spite of this word you did not believe the LORD your God"

God had taken the Hebrews from the dregs of captivity to the brink of successful conquest and freedom. All they had to do was believe. Their lack of faith and perspective caused them to falter. The people demanded that spies go into the land before they would attack. God had promised to deliver their foes to them sight unseen but the people paused and became fearful and cautious. They grossly underestimated God. The spies returned and told the people that there was an enemy in the land and he was large and ferocious. The Hebrews faltered and their fear grew. As their fear grew greater, their commitment to their calling shrunk. As a consequence of their lack of faith and commitment, they were condemned by God to wander in the wilderness for an entire generation. A second generation would be called upon to finish the task the first had begun.

DOCTRINE: BELGIC CONFESSION (1561)

ARTICLE 36, We believe that our gracious God, because of the depravity of mankind, hath appointed kings, princes, and magistrates, willing that the world should be governed by certain laws and policies; to the end that the dissoluteness of men might be restrained, and all things carried on among them with good order and decency. For this purpose he hath invested the magistracy with the sword, for the punishment of evil doers, and for the praise of them that do well. And their office is, not only to have regard unto and watch for the welfare of the civil state, but also that they protect the sacred ministry, and thus may remove and prevent all idolatry and false worship; that the kingdom of antichrist may be thus destroyed, and the Kingdom of Christ promoted. They must therefore, countenance the preaching of the word of the gospel everywhere, that God may be honored and worshipped by everyone, as He commands in His Word.

Moreover, it is the bounden duty of every one, of what state, quality, or condition he may be, to subject himself to the magistrates; to pay tribute, to show due honor and respect to them, and to obey them in all things which are not repugnant to the Word of God; to supplicate for them in their prayers, that God may rule and guide them in all their ways, and that we may lead a quiet and peaceable life in all godliness and honesty.

[9]

Question: **What do you think of those who sit by and do not strive with you against evil in these difficult times?**
Answer:
1. *Either they are not convinced of the necessity,*
2. *Or they are complacent in their convictions*
3. *Or they are self indulgent, loving money and ease more than God*
4. *Or they are faint-hearted Cowards*
5. *Or they are secret Enemies of God, all that is good, the liberties of our Republic, the United States of America.*

THOUGHTS FOR INSPIRATION:

"It is true that so far as wealth gives time for ideal ends and exercise to ideal energies, wealth is better than poverty and ought to be chosen. But wealth does this in only a portion of the actual cases. Elsewhere the desire to gain wealth and the fear to lose it are our chief breeders of cowardice and propagators of corruption. There must be thousands of conjunctures in which a wealth-bound man must be a slave, whilst a man for whom poverty has no terrors becomes a freeman." *William James*

"Mr. President, it is natural to man to indulge in the illusions of Hope. We are apt to shut our eyes against a painful truth, and listen to the song of that siren till she transforms us into beasts. Is this the part of wise men, engaged in a great and arduous struggle for liberty? Are we disposed to be of the number of those who, having eyes, see not, and having ears, hear not, the things which so nearly concern their temporal salvation? For my part, whatever anguish of spirit it may cost, I am willing to know the whole truth; to know the worst, and to provide for it...", "It is in vain, sir, to extenuate the matter. Gentlemen may cry peace, peace, but there is no peace. The war is actually begun. The next gale that sweeps from the north will bring to our ears the clash of resounding arms. Our brethren are already in the field. Why stand we here idle? What is it that gentlemen wish? What would they have? Is life so dear, or peace so sweet, as to be purchased at the price of chains and slavery? Forbid it, Almighty God! I know not what course others may take, but as for me, give me liberty, or give me death!" *Patrick Henry*

"We are expected to put the utmost energy, of every power that we have, into the service of our fellow men, never sparing ourselves, not condescending to think of what is going to happen to ourselves, but ready, if need be, to go to the utter length of self-sacrifice." *President Woodrow Wilson*

"For too long our culture has said, 'If it *feels* good, do it.' Now America is embracing a new ethic and a new creed: 'Let's roll.' In the sacrifice of soldiers, the fierce brotherhood of firefighters, and the bravery and generosity of ordinary citizens, we have glimpsed what a new culture of responsibility could look like. We want to be a nation that serves goals larger than self. We've been offered a unique opportunity, and we must not let this moment pass." *President George W. Bush,*

"Cowardice asks the question, 'Is it safe?' Expediency asks the question, 'Is it politic?' But conscience asks the question, 'Is it right?' And there comes a time when one must take a position that is neither safe, nor politic, nor popular but because conscience tells one it is right." *Dr. Martin Luther King, Jr.*

REFLECTION: RESOLUTION
The 1913 edition of Webster's Dictionary listed one definition of *resolve* as, *"To determine or decide in purpose; to make ready in mind; to fix; to settle."* A man must be resolved about certain issues in life. Liberty is no longer a matter for discussion but one for conviction and resolution. We have already resolved that men were created with certain rights given by their creator to life, liberty, and the pursuit of happiness. No longer do we wonder if those are worthy goals. They simply are. Men lacking resolve essentially lack both *commitment* and *courage* to defend those things that are necessary.

STUDY AND MEDIATION: NEHEMIAH 4:11-14

"And our enemies said, 'They will not know or see till we come among them and kill them and stop the work.' At that time the Jews who lived near them came from all directions and said to us ten times, "You must return to us." So in the lowest parts of the space behind the wall, in open places, I stationed the people by their clans, with their swords, their spears, and their bows. And I looked and arose and said to the nobles and to the officials and to the rest of the people, "Do not be afraid of them. Remember the Lord, who is great and awesome, and fight for your brothers, your sons, your daughters, your wives, and your homes."

In Nehemiah 4, half of the Jews in the city worked to rebuild the city walls that were torn down and the other half stood with spears in a constant state of vigilance ready for any attack that may come. Those surrounding Jerusalem had petitioned for peace but only on the condition that the Jews would stop their work in rebuilding the city. The Jews new that their commission was to rebuild and that there was no turning from that path. Their options were to capitulate and follow the designs of a foreign body or to be prepared and willing to fight for their own preservation. They chose to fight. So they worked with bricks in one hand and the sword in the other. Their commander, Nehemiah sums up the source of the confidence and inspiration to give themselves to their cause. Instead of being motivated by self-centered goals, or a fear of punishment, he said, *"Remember God who is your salvation. And remember who you are defending. There are those who would lead your family away from you. There are those who want to use you to accomplish their own goals. But God has called you to be something more. Stay the course, sacrifice for something greater than yourselves, give yourself to the defense of the nation God has established and the defense of your family. Have courage and do not shrink back, because of fear or love of life, from this hour of your testing."*

DOCTRINE: BELGIC CONFESSION

Article 24, We, believe that this true faith, being wrought in man by the hearing of the Word of God and the operation of the Holy Ghost, doth regenerate and make him a new man, causing him to live a new life, and freeing him from the bondage of sin. Therefore it is so far from being true, that this justifying faith makes men remiss in a pious and holy life, that on the contrary without it they would never do anything out of love to God, but only out of self-love or fear of damnation.

[10]

Question: **What dangers are such pacifists in?**
Answer:
1. *God takes special notice of their disposition and carriage, and will deal with them accordingly.*
2. *In God's account all such are enemies; they that are not with him are against him.*
3. *They deserve neither respect nor protection from Church or State.*
4. *They are in danger to be spit out of Christ's mouth, Revelation 3:16, "So, because you are lukewarm, and neither hot nor cold, I will spit you out of my mouth."*
5. *They are directly under the dreadful curse which the Angel of the Lord denounced against Meroz, Judges 5:23. "Curse Meroz, says the angel of the LORD, curse its inhabitants thoroughly, because they did not come to the help of the LORD, to the help of the LORD against the mighty."*

THOUGHTS FOR INSPIRATION:

"Our lives begin to end the day we become silent about things that matter."
                                              Martin Luther King, Jr

"Moral courage is the most valuable and usually the most absent characteristic in men."   *General George S. Patton, Jr*

"Beware lest in your anxiety to avoid war you obtain a master."
                                              Demosthenes

"The fact that slaughter [battle] is a horrifying spectacle must make us take war more seriously, but [it does] not provide an excuse for gradually blunting our swords in the name of humanity. Sooner or later someone will come along with a sharp sword and hack off our arms." *Carl von Clausewitz*

"Ours is neither a perfect nor a perfectible world; it is a theater of perpetual conflict in which the prize goes to the strong. Peace through war; security through strength"   Excerpt from *Redemptive Violence*,
                                              Walter Wink

"Evil men do not understand justice,
  but those who seek the LORD understand it completely."   *Proverbs 28:5*

REFLECTION: JUSTICE

In his writing, *The Republic*, Plato treats justice as an ideal or foundational virtue, which means that almost every ethical issue somehow or another relates to the notion of justice. If a man lied for example, Plato connects that vice to the larger issue of justice. Modern thinking sees justice more as a legal issue. You may be a liar yourself, but if you don't cheat or steal from others, you may be considered *just*. Justice is about truth. It is about setting things right. Perhaps we have compartmetalized our virtue into unrecognizable portions. Maybe it is time to take an account of the whole man again rather than his individual components. Comprehensive character development should once again be our goal rather than individual skills, utilitarianism and situational ethics.

STUDY AND MEDITATION: NUMBERS 31:7-18

"They warred against Midian, as the LORD commanded Moses, and killed every male. They killed the kings of Midian with the rest of their slain, Evi, Rekem, Zur, Hur, and Reba, the five kings of Midian. And they also killed Balaam the son of Beor with the sword. And the people of Israel took captive the women of Midian and their little ones, and they took as plunder all their cattle, their flocks, and all their goods. All their cities in the places where they lived, and all their encampments, they burned with fire, and took all the spoil and all the plunder, both of man and of beast. Then they brought the captives and the plunder and the spoil to Moses, and to Eleazar the priest, and to the congregation of the people of Israel, at the camp on the plains of Moab by the Jordan at Jericho.

Moses and Eleazar the priest and all the chiefs of the congregation went to meet them outside the camp. And Moses was angry with the officers of the army, the commanders of thousands and the commanders of hundreds, who had come from service in the war. Moses said to them, "Have you let all the women live? Behold, these, on Balaam's advice, caused the people of Israel to act treacherously against the LORD in the incident of Peor, and so the plague came among the congregation of the LORD. Now therefore, kill every male among the little ones, and kill every woman who has known man by lying with him. But all the young girls who have not known man by lying with him keep alive for yourselves."

Numbers 31 describes the justice of God meted out against the Midianites because they had seduced the people of God to worship idols and participate in sexual immorality. That seduction had violated the divinity and honor of

Jehovah. God commanded His people to treat them as enemies and kill them. Their sin had reached its full measure and their time of judgment had come. Moses had 1000 men from each tribe equipped for war. He sent them along with Phinehas the son of the high priest because the war was a holy war pitting the people of God against the enemies of God. A great battle followed in which the Midianites were taken by surprise and completely routed. All the adult males were slain. The women and children were led away as prisoners and their cattle and belongings were taken as spoils of war. The towns and villages were burned to the ground. The people of Midian were erased from history.

Moses was actually angry that the women were taken alive because they had caused the people of God to switch from true worship to idolatry. He commanded that all the male children should be slain and that only the young women that had never been with a man should be spared. The objective was not cruelty or barbarism but that the whole nation was to be eliminated because of their rebellion against God, false worship and degenerative influence. God wanted to preserve His people against the deluding influence of false worship.

From this we learn that there comes a time when the rebellion of man and his offense against God reaches an end. God's patience will be exhausted and His judgment will begin. That judgment may be executed by men through war. Romans 12:19 teaches, *"Beloved, never avenge yourselves, but leave it to the wrath of God, for it is written, "Vengeance is mine, I will repay, says the Lord."* This passage doesn't teach us never to wage war but instead, to make sure that the war we wage is warranted by God's Word which is living and active and sharper than any double-edged sword. The weapons of warfare for God's people today are spiritual. The Word of God transforms the heart of men and renews the world. Nonetheless, God places the sword of justice in the hands of the civil government and all men everywhere are expected to stand for justice and the protection of Liberty for the sake of the Gospel and the peace of His people.

DOCTRINE: WESTMINSTER CONFESSION OF FAITH

XXIII.1, God, the supreme Lord and King of all the world, hath ordained civil magistrates, to be, under Him, over the people, for His own glory, and the public good: and, to this end, hath armed them with the power of the sword, for the defense and encouragement of them that are good, and for the punishment of evil doers.

[11]

Question: **What do you say to those Christians who align themselves to join with or defend the enemies of God and the Liberty of men?**
Answer:

1.　*I say that they of all other men are least worthy to carry the name "Christian" since they have positioned themselves against the cause of Christ.*
2.　*I say that they serve the cause of the Antichrist, the agent of evil, oppression, death, and darkness.*
3.　*That they are a shame and a blemish to the name of religion.*
4.　*That none of their weapons shall prosper, Isaiah 54:17.*
5.　*That God will utterly undo them, Zephaniah 3:19.*
6.　*That they share in the responsibility and will come under judgment for all the blood that has been shed.*
7.　*That they are in the highway to perdition in need of repentance.*
8.　*That the judgment of God for their treason against righteousness will come upon them more quickly than they imagine.*

THOUGHTS FOR INSPIRATION

"The man who pauses on the paths of treason, halts on a quicksand, the first step engulfs him."　　　　　　　　　*Aaron Hill, Henry V (act I, sc. 1)*

"Is there not some chosen curse, Some hidden thunder in the stores of heaven, red with uncommon wrath, to blast the man who owes his greatness to his country's ruin?"　　　　　　　*Joseph Addison, Cato (act I, sc. 1)*

"Treason is like diamonds; there is nothing to be made by the small trader"
　　　　　　　　　　　　　　　　　　　Douglas Jerrold

"Honor is like an island, rugged and without a beach; once we have left it, we can never return."　　　　　　　　　*Nicholas Boileau*

"You can discover what your enemy fears most by observing the means he uses to frighten you."　　　　　　　　　*Eric Hoffer*

REFLECTION: HONOR

The origins of our word, *honor* can be traced back to an Irish word which originally meant *face* (from the Old Celtic 'eniequos'). We get a sense of this in the phrase, *"Saving face..."* Since the concept of honor is so closely associated with *face*, [i.e., guarding our reputation in the eyes of the community], honor and dishonor find their anchors in the community more than in the individual codes or creeds that characterize modern thinking. Honor is both an adjective and an adverb. As an adverb, we behave honorably. We speak honorably. And as an adjective, it is a quality we possess. We may be an honorable person. Usually honor is conferred by others to an individual. Honor is earned, rather than claimed.

STUDY AND MEDITATION: 2 CHRONICLES 29:6-9

"For our fathers have been unfaithful and have done what was evil in the sight of the LORD our God. They have forsaken him and have turned away their faces from the habitation of the LORD and turned their backs. They also shut the doors of the vestibule and put out the lamps and have not burned incense or offered burnt offerings in the Holy Place to the God of Israel. Therefore the wrath of the LORD came on Judah and Jerusalem, and he has made them an object of horror, of astonishment, and of hissing, as you see with your own eyes. For behold, our fathers have fallen by the sword, and our sons and our daughters and our wives are in captivity for this."

The King of Judah, Hezekiah was a righteous man who began with an honest assessment of Judah's woes. The beleaguered nation had been racked with invasions and war. They were laid waste and their resources were drained. The government wasn't able to generate the needed revenue to continue the struggle under those circumstances. Hezekiah pointed out to the people that they had turned away from God under the previous king, his father, King Ahaz. Worship was neglected in the extreme and the nation was under the severe judgment of God. Hezekiah knew that the only way to save the nation was to return to God: first, with a request for forgiveness and then with a commitment to never neglect His proper worship and service in the future. He devised measures of national reform at the beginning of his reign to transform people long trained by idolatry. There is a special sort of courage that few possess to speak the truth in a dangerously depraved time of treason against God.

DOCTRINE: WESTMINSTER CONFESSION OF FAITH

XXXIII.3, As Christ would have us to be certainly persuaded that there shall be a day of judgment, both to deter all men from sin, and for the greater consolation of the godly in their adversity; so will He have that day unknown to men, that they may shake off all carnal security, and be always watchful, because they know not at what hour the Lord will come; and may be ever prepared to say, Come, Lord Jesus come quickly, Amen.

[12]

Question: **What is the reason that we seem to stand alone in our battles against evil?**
Answer:
1. *There are many that would appear both civilized and honest on the surface but we find underneath the public image that they are self-serving and uncommitted to the common good.*
2. *Many would prefer to join with us in our resistance against evil but fear for their own safety and so either sit passively or compromise with our enemies.*
3. *Many, desiring prosperity more than justice, have made financial gains from the war against evil and would stand to lose their profits if our enemies were defeated.*
4. *Many have been retained in power because of the threat of evil against their countries and would lose their positions of influence and rule if our enemies are defeated.*
5. *Many are genuinely threatened by those of good character. Having dwelled for so long in the shadows of bribery and injustice, they discover they unwittingly allied themselves to evil before the war began.*
6. *Many misunderstand the nature of this conflict assuming its ends to be material and political rather than moral and spiritual.*

THOUGHTS FOR INSPIRIATION:
"One should never allow chaos to develop in order to avoid going to war, because one does not avoid a war but instead puts it off to his disadvantage."
Nicolo Machiavelli, The Prince, 3

"Let me not pray to be sheltered from dangers but to be fearless in facing them. Let me not beg for the stilling of my pain, but for the heart to conquer it. Let me not look for allies in life's battlefield but to my own strength. Let me not cave in."
Rabindranath Tagor

"All that is essential for the triumph of evil is that good men do nothing."
Edmund Burke

"In war there is no prize for the runner-up."   *General Omar Bradley*

"When bad men combine, the good must associate else they will fall one by one, an un-pitied sacrifice in a contemptible struggle."   *Edmund Burke*

"If ye love wealth better than liberty, the tranquility of servitude better than the animating contest of freedom, go home from us in peace. We ask not your counsels or arms. Crouch down and lick the hands which feed you. May your chains set lightly upon you, and may posterity forget ye were our countrymen."
                                                            Samuel Adams

"If you will not fight for the right when you can easily win without bloodshed, if you will not fight when victory will be sure and not so costly, you may come to the moment when you will have to fight with all the odds against you and only a precarious chance of survival. There may be a worse case. You may have to fight when there is no chance of victory, because it is better to perish than to live as slaves."   *Winston Churchill*

"Those who expect to reap the blessings of freedom must, like men, undergo the fatigue of supporting it."   *Thomas Paine*

"An appeaser is one who feeds a crocodile, hoping it will eat him last."
                                                        Winston Churchill

"Right is more precious than peace."   *Woodrow Wilson*

"We will remember not the words of our enemies, but the silence of our friends.
                                                    Martin Luther King, Jr.

REFLECTION: CONVICTION
We most often hear of a conviction when someone is sentenced for a crime. That legal use of the term is not far from understanding the convictions held by men. Essentially, conviction is a judgment or decision, a firmly held belief that has been decided after careful contemplation. While it is true, that many in our day avoid careful contemplation, that doesn't remove the need for convictions. Without convictions, what is it that men fight for or celebrate? If we hold no convictions, or if we are not certain about anything, then how can we decide what we are to do? There comes a time that we no longer keep all options open standing paralyzed by indecision. There comes a time in the lives of all men when they *must* arrive at an educated and reasonable decision, a course of action, a conviction. Convictions form those principles that we are unwilling to compromise. They form our axioms for life.

STUDY AND MEDITATION: VARIOUS

"For though we walk in the flesh, we are not waging war according to the flesh. For the weapons of our warfare are not of the flesh but have divine power to destroy strongholds. We destroy arguments and every lofty opinion raised against the knowledge of God, and take every thought captive to obey Christ, being ready to punish every disobedience, when your obedience is complete."

1 Corinthians 10:4-6

"When you draw near to a city to fight against it, offer terms of peace to it. And if it responds to you peaceably and it opens to you, then all the people who are found in it shall do forced labor for you and shall serve you. But if it makes no peace with you, but makes war against you, then you shall besiege it."

Deuteronomy 20:10-12

When the people of God were advancing against those who opposed them, they were instructed to call out for peace or offer their enemies an opportunity to surrender and submit before the battle. This was not a truce or an opportunity to ignore or set aside the injustice that brought on the war. It was an opportunity for the enemy to be defeated without dying. If the enemies of God, of justice, and of righteousness refused to relent and submit, then the people of God were to march against them and utterly destroy them just as a human cancer must be removed from a body to restore health. This is the same as with sin. It must not be spared or indulged. It must be repented of and destroyed, for Jesus has said that we must be holy as our heavenly Father is holy. He also said that a tree will be known by its fruit.

DOCTRINE: CANONS OF DORT (1619)

Head II Article 1, God is not only supremely merciful, but also supremely just. And His justice requires (as He hath revealed Himself in His Word), that our sins committed against His infinite majesty should be punished, not only with temporal, but with eternal punishment, both in body and soul; which we cannot escape unless satisfaction be made to the justice of God.

[13]

Question. **What is your chief aim in war?**
Answer.

1. *The confrontation and destruction of Babylon[6] in whatever form she may arise in whatever epoch of history, that city of evil that opposes all righteousness and godliness, returning to it what it has served to others. Psalm 137:8 "O daughter of Babylon, doomed to be destroyed, blessed shall he be who repays you with what you have done to us!"*
2. *To advance all that is good in the Kingdom of God.*
3. *To bring the light of truth to the dark corners of the world.*
4. *To bring the enemies of God and the enemies of our Nation to justice.*
5. *To uphold our national sovereignty, provide for the common defense, to protect our national government.*
6. *To maintain that freedom of religion that was so cherished by our founding fathers.*

THOUGHTS FOR INSPIRATION:

"No one can terrorize a whole nation, unless we are all his accomplices."
Edward R. Murrow

"They who would give up an essential liberty for temporary security, deserve neither liberty or security."
Benjamin Franklin

"The purpose of all war is peace."
Saint Augustine

"It is only those who have neither fired a shot nor heard the shrieks and groans of the wounded who cry aloud for blood, more vengeance, more desolation. War is hell."
William T. Sherman

"You are either with us, or you are with the terrorists."
President George H.W. Bush

"Terror is not a new weapon. Throughout history it has been used by those who could not prevail, either by persuasion or example. But inevitably they fail, either because men are not afraid to die for a life worth living, or because the terrorists themselves came to realize that free men cannot be frightened by threats, and that aggression would meet its own response. And it is in the light of that history that

every nation today should know, be he friend or foe, that the United States has both the will and the weapons to join free men in standing up to their responsibilities."
President John F. Kennedy

"We are engaged mainly in a struggle for the soul of this new century. Victory for our vision depends upon winning the fight we're in against terrorism, on spreading the benefits, and reducing the burdens of the modern world, on changes in poor nations themselves that will make progress possible, and finally, on developing a global level of consciousness about what our responsibilities to each other are and what our relationships ought to be."
President William J. Clinton

"America has entered a great struggle that tests our strength, and even more our resolve. Our nation is patient and steadfast. We continue to pursue the terrorists in cities and camps and caves across the earth. We are joined by a great coalition of nations to rid the world of terror. And we will not allow any terrorist or tyrant to threaten civilization with weapons of mass murder. Now and in the future, Americans will live as free people, not in fear, and never at the mercy of any foreign plot or power."
President George Walker Bush,
New York, New York, Sep. 11, 2002

REFLECTION: HOPE

Hope is the synthesis of *desire* and *expectation.* Conversely, hopelessness is a desire without expectation of success. Indifference is an expectation without a desire. As long as men follow God and seek to do His will, God will accomplish all that He has intended to do since the beginning. Whether it is to bring the walls of Jericho down or to miraculously save an overwhelmed army, if we desire to do God's will and expect God to accomplish His will, then there is always hope.

STUDY AND MEDITATION: NEHEMIAH 4:14

"And I looked and arose and said to the nobles and to the officials and to the rest of the people, 'Do not be afraid of them. Remember the Lord, who is great and awesome, and fight for your brothers, your sons, your daughters, your wives, and your homes.'"

Nehemiah explains that because of the constant threat to the builders working on the city walls and fortifications, half of them had to be pulled off of the construction and armed for defense. With only half of the men working and half of the men defending, neither was fully equipped and manned to accomplish the mission. Not only did fatigue begin to take a toll but fear of being overwhelmed also plagued their minds as the enemy didn't have to focus their resources but on one task, attacking the Israelites. Nehemiah encourages the people by refocusing them from the problems they face and the enormous odds stacked against them. He calls them to remember why they are there, who is depending on them and the supreme and all powerful God who will not let His purpose nor His people be undone, and to their expectations that God will give them success. With renewed confidence, faith, and purpose the men stood their ground and were victorious against their enemies.

DOCTRINE: CANONS OF DORT

Head II Article 9, This purpose proceeding from everlasting love towards the elect has from the beginning of the world to this day been powerfully accomplished, and will henceforward still continue to be accomplished, notwithstanding all the ineffectual opposition of the gates of hell, so that the elect in due time may be gathered together into one, and that there never may be wanting a Church composed of believers, the foundation of which is laid in the blood of Christ, which may steadfastly love and faithfully serve Him as their Savior, who as a bridegroom for his bride, laid down His life for them upon the cross, and which may celebrate His praises here and through all eternity.

[14]

Question: **Do you have any hope of prevailing in your cause?**
Answer: We have encouragements enough to assure us of good success: there are many arguments to confirm our hope.

1. *From the justness and goodness of the Cause itself.*
2. *From the course that has been taken.*
3. *From the condition and commitment of those that are engaged in the war.*
4. *From the poor quality of our enemies in both their moral virtue and their preparation for battle.*
5. *From the cheerfulness of most men's spirits who have committed themselves to the defense of our national cause.*
6. *From the many victories already secured.*
7. *From our National heritage and the oaths which all who are in the war have taken.*
8. *From God's Providence and good care of His people.*

THOUGHTS FOR INSPIRATION:
"The world's a stage, where God's omnipotence, His justice, knowledge, love, and providence do act the parts."   *Guillaume de Salluste*

"I like to see a man proud of the place in which he lives. I like to see a man live so that his place will be proud of him."   *Abraham Lincoln*

"America is much more than a geographical fact. It is a political and moral fact - the first community in which men set out in principle to institutionalize freedom, responsible government, and human equality."   *Adlai Stevenson*

"This, then, is the state of the union: free and restless, growing and full of hope. So it was in the beginning. So it shall always be, while God is willing, and we are strong enough to keep the faith."   *Lyndon B. Johnson*

"My God! How little do my countrymen know what precious blessings they are in possession of, and which no other people on earth enjoy!"
                Thomas Jefferson

"To the dim and bewildered vision of humanity, God's care is more evident in some instances than in others; and upon such instances men seize, and call them providences. It is well that they can; but it would be gloriously better if they could believe that the whole matter is one grand providence."
                George Macdonald

"Trust in the providence of God is not a heaven-sent formula for the indolent, not a way of bypassing responsibility with regard to social and material concerns ... you have to take on the affairs that come your way, knowing that they come from God and must be steered back again to him."
                Hubert von Zeller

REFLECTION: CONFIDENCE
Man has struggled with two perspectives. He learns to have a confidence in his own hands, in his own wit, in his own wisdom. Then, when that fails him, he despairs. That is why man is comfortable disregarding God until he is in the foxholes of life. When all is fair and good man is comfortable with himself but when the world looms large before him and events begin to overwhelm him he wants to then call out to God and ask Him to take charge of life. Far greater the man and superior his thinking who understands that God has a plan for all of *His* creation and that *He* is working to move *His* creation towards that end which *He* has ordained and which is for the good of all *His* people.

STUDY AND MEDITATION: VARIOUS
Proverbs 21:31, *"The horse is made ready for the day of battle, but the victory belongs to the LORD."*

Deuteronomy 20:4, *"for the LORD your God is he who goes with you to fight for you against your enemies, to give you the victory."*

Jeremiah 29:11, *"For I know the plans I have for you, declares the LORD, plans for wholeness and not for evil, to give you a future and a hope."*

DOCTRINE: BELGIC CONFESSION

ARTICLE 13, We believe that the same God, after He had created all things, did not forsake them, or give them up to fortune or chance, but that He rules and governs them according to His holy will, so that nothing happens in this world without His appointment; nevertheless, God neither is the author of, nor can be charged with, the sins which are committed. For His power and goodness are so great and incomprehensible, that He orders and executes His work in the most excellent and just manner, even then when devils and wicked men act unjustly. And as to what He doth surpassing human understanding, we will not curiously inquire into it further than our capacity will admit of; but with the greatest humility and reverence adore the righteous judgments of God which are hid from us, contenting ourselves that we are disciples of Christ, to learn only those things which He has revealed to us in His Word without transgressing these limits.

This doctrine affords us unspeakable consolation, since we are taught thereby that *nothing can befall us by chance*, but by the direction of our most gracious and heavenly Father, who watches over us with a paternal care, keeping all creatures so under His power that not a hair of our head (for they are all numbered), nor a sparrow, can fall to the ground, without the will of our Father, in whom we do entirely trust; being persuaded that He so restrains the devil and all our enemies that, without His will and permission, they cannot hurt us. *And therefore we reject that damnable error of the Epicureans, who say that God regards nothing, but leaves all things to chance.*

[15]

Question: **Explain the hopes you possess from the goodness of the Cause.**
Answer:
1. *A good Cause puts life and courage into the hearts of men.*
2. *A good Cause has God as an advocate.*
3. *A good Cause discourages and intimidates the enemies of righteousness.*
4. *A good Cause will undoubtedly prevail in the end.*

THOUGHTS FOR INSPIRATION:
"In a just cause the weak will beat the strong."   *Sophocles*

"The humblest citizen of all the land when clad in the armor of a righteous cause, is stronger than all the hosts of Error."   *William Jennings Bryan*

"Ours is an abiding faith in the cause of human freedom. We know it is God's cause."   *Thomas E. Dewey*

"Respectable men and women content with good and easy living are missing some of the most important things in life. Unless you give; yourself to some great cause you haven't even begun to live."   *William P. Merrill*

"The silent majority distrusts people who believe in causes."   *Brian Moore*

"No cause is helpless if it is just. Errors, no matter how popular, carry the seeds of their own destruction."   *John W. Scoville*

"A bad cause will never be supported but by bad means and bad men."
                    Thomas Paine

REFLECTION: IDEALISM
Idealism is the opposite of cynicism. Idealism is a belief in good and noble goals and a habit of pursuing them. An idealist can see things in their *ideal* form no matter what their condition at present. An idealist is far from naive. An idealist believes all things good are possible or at least are worthy of pursuit.

STUDY AND MEDITATION: 2 SAMUEL 22:1-4
And David spoke to the LORD the words of this song on the day when the LORD delivered him from the hand of all his enemies, and from the hand of Saul. He said,
    "The LORD is my rock and my fortress and my deliverer,
    my God, my rock, in whom I take refuge,
    my shield, and the horn of my salvation,
    my stronghold and my refuge,
    my savior; you save me from violence.
    I call upon the LORD, who is worthy to be praised,
    and I am saved from my enemies."

After King David was rescued from the murderous attempts on his life by Saul, David sang a song to God reflecting his understanding that it was God and God alone that saved his life. Several of the features presented in the song can help us in times of despair when we call out to God as well.

- *God is my Rock* –my protection of inaccessible height
- *God is my Fortress & Shield* –He is my protection and defense against assault
- *God is my Deliverer* –The one who makes it so that I can "go forth" from where I am.
- *He is "My God"*–The object of my faith and worship. He is living and active.
- *God is the Horn of my Salvation* –The horn is the means of calling for attack or defense and is the symbol of summoned power and strength in action.
- *God is my Stronghold* –A tower of strength that stands firm against an attack

DOCTRINE: SECOND HELVETIC CONFESSION

XVI.1, Christian faith is not an opinion or human persuasion, but a sure trust, and an evident and steadfast assent of the mind; it is a most sure comprehension of the truth of God, set forth in the Scriptures and in the Apostles' Creed; yea, and of God Himself, the chief blessedness; and especially of God's promise, and of Christ, who is the consummation of all the promises. And this faith is the mere gift of God, because God alone of His power does give it to His elect, according to measure; and that when to whom, and how much He will; and that by His Holy Spirit, through the means of preaching the gospel and of faithful prayer. This faith has also its measures of increase, which, unless they were likewise given of God, the apostles would never have said, "Lord, increase our faith" (Luke 17:5).

[16]

Question: **Explain the reasons you believe you will prevail and show what hope you have from the goodness of the Cause.**
Answer:

  1. *A good Cause puts life and courage into men's hearts.*
  2. *A good Cause has GOD ever siding with it.*
  3. *A good Cause daunts and dismays the adverse party.*
  4. *A good Cause will undoubtedly prevail in the end.*

THOUGHTS FOR INSPIRATION:

"Respectable men and women content with good and easy living are missing some of the most important things in life. Unless you give yourself to some great cause you haven't even begun to live." *William P. Merrill*

"We are all ready to be savage in some cause. The difference between a good man and a bad one is the choice of the cause." *William James*

"No man is worth his salt who is not ready at all times to risk his well-being, to risk his body, to risk his life, in a great cause." *Theodore Roosevelt*

"The probability that we may fail in the struggle ought not to deter us from the support of a cause we believe to be just." *Abraham Lincoln*

"Once a man has made a commitment to a way of life, he puts the greatest strength in the world behind him. It's something we call heart power. Once a man has made this commitment, nothing will stop him short of success."
Vincent Lombardi

"The liberties of our country, the freedom of our civil Constitution, are worth defending at all hazards; and it is our duty to defend them against all attacks. We have received them as a fair inheritance from our worthy ancestors: they purchased them for us with toil and danger and expense of treasure and blood, and transmitted them to us with care and diligence. It will bring an everlasting mark of infamy on the present generation, enlightened as it is, if we should suffer them to be wrested from us by violence without a struggle, or to be cheated out of them by the artifices of false and designing men." *Samuel Adams*

"Confidence... thrives on honesty, on honor, on the sacredness of obligations, on faithful protection and on unselfish performance. Without them it cannot live." *Franklin D. Roosevelt*

REFLECTION: CONFIDENCE

Confidence can be as tricky as it is simple. It is nothing more than *food-faith* or an *assurance* that a predictable reaction will come from an anticipated action. When we sit in a chair we have confidence that the legs will hold us up, else, we wouldn't sit in the chair. As we grow, we receive an education and then when we enter our vocational fields, we are given additional training or equipment as we need it to accomplish our mission. With each success our confidence grows. That is not a place where confidence is tested however. When we are taught what we need to know and given all the resources necessary to accomplish a task or a goal, there is no great claim to virtue in believing the predictable will come to pass. When we are called on to reflect on all that God has done and to trust that He is able to do far and above anything we can imagine, and then we are called on to act in faith without the adequate resources that guarantee success by our own natural abilities, then we have learned the virtue of confidence.

STUDY AND MEDITATION: JEREMIAH 11:20

"The LORD made it known to me and I knew; then you showed me their deeds. But I was like a gentle lamb led to the slaughter. I did not know it was against me they devised schemes, saying, 'Let us destroy the tree with

its fruit, let us cut him off from the land of the living, that his name be remembered no more.' But, O LORD of hosts, who judges righteously, who tests the heart and the mind, let me see your vengeance upon them, for to you have I committed my cause."

Because of the prophet Jeremiah's condemnation of the people's sins, even his friends began to plot against him. Jeremiah knew nothing about the evil plots against his life until God revealed it to him. Then Jeremiah equates his own purpose with the cause of God. Had he not been speaking out about the things that offend God, they would not have been upset and plotted against him. Jeremiah understood that his purpose for living was to carry out the cause of the Lord which was Jeremiah's cause as well.

For all who are in God, our purpose is continually being changed into His purpose. Our mind is being conformed to the mind of Christ. Our battles become less about ourselves and more about Him who called us from death to life. We become less and He becomes more.

DOCTRINE: WESTMINSTER CONFESSION OF FAITH

IX.4, When God converts a sinner, and translates him into the state of grace, He freeth him from his natural bondage under sin; and, by His grace alone, enables him freely to will and to do that which is spiritually good; yet so, as that by reason of his remaining corruption, he doth not perfectly, nor only, will that which is good, but doth also will that which is evil.

[17]

Question: **What is your encouragement from the course that has been taken?**
Answer:
1. *In that all fair and Christian alternatives have been considered and attempted before we took up arms.*
2. *In that the will of the Lord was generally and earnestly sought before the business of war was undertaken.*
3. *In that it was undertaken with good advice, and is guided by a multitude of Counselors.*
4. *In that it is still followed with the prayers and supplications of all the faithful in the Land.*

THOUGHTS FOR INSPIRATION:

"Where no counsel is, the people fall: but in the multitude of counselors there is safety."   *Proverbs 11:14*

"In great straits and when hope is small, the boldest counsels are the safest."
Titus Livy, Annales (XXV, 38)

"Wise leaders generally have wise Counselors because it takes a wise person themselves to distinguish them."   *Diogenes of Sinope*

"They that will not be Counseled, cannot be helped. If you do not hear reason she will rap you on the knuckles."   *Benjamin Franklin*

"He that gives good advice, builds with one hand; he that gives good counsel and example, builds with both; but he that gives good admonition and bad example, builds with one hand and pulls down with the other."
Francis Bacon

"Peace if possible but truth at any rate."   *Martin Luther*

REFLECTON: HUMILITY

"Humility makes the virtues discreet unself-conscious, almost self-effacing. Humility is not, however, a lack of awareness; it is the extreme awareness of the limits of all virtue and of one's own limits as well."[7] For a man to remain humble, he has to prize truth above appearance. He has to deal honestly with his limitations and engage them to improve them. If a man is more concerned with hiding his faults from others, then they remain his weakness. Pride is said to go before a fall. If a child is afraid for people to know he can't yet walk, then he will never learn.

STUDY AND MEDITATION: PSALM 25:8-10

"Good and upright is the LORD; therefore he instructs sinners in the way. He leads the humble in what is right, and teaches the humble his way. All the paths of the LORD are steadfast love and faithfulness, for those who keep His covenant and His testimonies."

When we say that the Lord is upright, we mean that He is acting according to His promise. The *path* or *the way*, are the paths of His providence. God has a plan for His creation, He has already determined how history will flow and culminate in the end. It is ours to remain in His will and participate in that plan of history. Where God has revealed His will, that is the right way or path that we must follow. He has condescended to us in order to teach us the way that leads to life. When the Psalmists adds, *"For those who keep His covenant and His testimonies..."* we are reminded that the good things

God has planned for us are only for those who consistently, courageously, and sacrificially remain centered in His providential plan. There are no other paths that will lead to happiness and satisfaction. Peace can be purchased only for a short time and the violence that is postponed will grow more violent as it cures and matures. To those who are self-righteous and think they depend on God for nothing, he will force Himself against their will and they will learn not of His blessings, but of His righteous indignation and wrath. God will reward those who carefully guard what they have learned and seek His paths to truth and peace.

DOCTRINE: SECOND HELVETIC CONFESSION

X.5, And when the Lord was asked whether there were few that should be saved, He does not answer and tell them that few or many should be saved or damned, but rather He exhorts every man to *"strive to enter in at the strait gate"* (Luke 13:24): as if He should say, It is not for you rashly to inquire of these matters, but rather to endeavor that you may enter into heaven by the strait way.

[18]

Question; **What has convinced you that our cause is morally right and necessary to fight for?**
Answer:
1. *It is reassuring that the faithful and godly ministers of this country do support and side with our cause.*
2. *The other soldiers are generally full of courage and resolution to do what is right.*
3. *There is an important and overt emphasis on the religious and spiritual nature of our soldiers.*

THOUGHTS FOR INSPIRATION:

"It is fatal to enter any war without the will to win it." *Gen. Douglas MacArthur*

"The architects of this wickedness will find no safe harbor in this world. We will chase our enemies to the furthest corners of this Earth. It must be war without quarter, pursuit without rest, victory without qualification."

Rep. Tom Delay
Former Majority Whip, US House of Representatives

"I count him braver who overcomes his desires than him who conquers his enemies; for the hardest victory is over self."   *Aristotle*

"War is an ugly thing, but not the ugliest of things. The decayed and degraded state of moral and patriotic feeling which thinks that nothing is worth war is much worse. The person who has nothing for which he is willing to fight, nothing which is more important than his own personal safety, is a miserable creature, and has no chance of being free unless made or kept so by the exertions of better men than himself."   *John Stuart Mill*

"Confidence is contagious. So is lack of confidence."   *Vince Lombardi*

"It is in vain, sir, to extenuate the matter. Gentlemen may cry, Peace, Peace— but there is no peace. The war is actually begun! The next gale that sweeps from the north will bring to our ears the clash of resounding arms! Our brethren are already in the field! Why stand we here idle? What is it that gentlemen wish? What would they have? Is life so dear, or peace so sweet, as to be purchased at the price of chains and slavery? Forbid it, Almighty God! I know not what course others may take; but as for me, give me liberty or give me death!"   *Patrick Henry, March, 23, 1775*

REFLECTION: DISCERNMENT

How can we know when we must accept the misfortunes of war? A discerning person is one with understanding combined with the ability to discriminate and sort information related to the area under consideration. It is more than knowing "what" something is. It is also knowing what to *"do"* with the knowledge. Discernment is a sure sign that a man is maturing and that his *reason* is beginning to master his *desires* in order to guide his *will.* Jesus acknowledged as much when he lamented man's double mindedness in Matthew 26:41 and the Apostle James warned about the war that takes place within a man (James 1:8, 4:8). This inner war must be won for discernment to emerge as a virtue of reason.

Often our decisions are not between something good and bad but between two goods or the lesser of two evils. Mature and rational thinking, i.e., *discernment,* enables an individual to know which of the two he should choose and to anticipate the results from his choice. Discernment is a virtue because the virtues are concerned with what makes a man good in his conduct. Discernment gives a man the ability to see what will make life good and what will not and to gather from that understanding of what he should do.

STUDY AND MEDITATION: DEUTERONOMY 20:1-4

"When you go out to war against your enemies, and see horses and chariots and an army larger than your own, you shall not be afraid of them, for the

LORD your God is with you, who brought you up out of the land of Egypt. And when you draw near to the battle, the priest shall come forward and speak to the people and shall say to them, 'Hear, O Israel, today you are drawing near for battle against your enemies: let not your heart faint. Do not fear or panic or be in dread of them, for the LORD your God is he who goes with you to fight for you against your enemies, to give you the victory.'"

When the Israelites went into war, they were faced with a superior army. The light infantry of the Israelites faced Cavalry and chariots. Yet they were told to not be alarmed because they had not only the promise of God which is enough for any man, but the historical evidence from their Exodus from Egypt that God secures the victory for those who are in His will and following His path. The Israelites came to know the victorious power of God in the face of overwhelming odds. How much more has God proven Himself for us now that we have the victory won by Christ. Not only in the fields of battle do we learn to lean on the Lord's strength but in our battle for personal holiness and virtue we find our fleshly desires will overwhelm us if we do not lean on God for strength and victory. The implements of the world in our spiritual battle are formidable. The allure of the flesh, the ease of wealth, the satisfaction of status. But none of these give us peace. Only Christ has won that peace just as He has secured our victory on the fields of battle, He has purchased our peace with God.

DOCTRINE: SECOND HELVETIC CONFESSION
V.3, We, in all dangers and casualties of life, call on Him alone, and that by the mediation of the only Mediator, and our intercessor, Jesus Christ. For it is expressly commanded us, *"Call upon Me in the day of trouble: I will deliver thee, and thou shalt glorify Me"* (Psalm 50:15). Moreover, the Lord has made a most large promise, saying, *"Whatsoever ye shall ask the Father,... He shall give it you"* (John 16:23); and again, *"Come unto Me, all ye that labor and are heavy laden, and I will give you rest"* (Matthew 11:28). And seeing it is written, *"How then shall they call on Him in whom they have not believed?"* (Romans 10:14), and we do believe in God alone; therefore we call upon Him only, and that through Christ. *"For there is one God,"* says the apostle, *"and one mediator between God and men, the man Christ Jesus"* (1 Timothy 2:5). Again, *"If any man sin, we have an advocate with the Father, Jesus Christ the righteous,"* etc. (1 John 2:1).

[19]

Question: **What encouragement in this war do you receive from considering the moral lax and unrighteous purposes of your enemies?**
Answer: *We may conclude that God will not prosper them.*
1. *Because they are for the most part irreligious cultists and atheists, with whom we have to deal.*
2. *Because they are Blasphemers against God.*
3. *Because they are for the most part inhumane, barbarous and cruel.*
4. *Because they are enemies to God, and the power of goodness; and therefore the Lord will scatter them.*
5. *Because they are willing to attack the innocent and defenseless without provocation.*
6. *Because their goal and aim is death, ours in battle, their own in martyrdom.*

THOUGHTS FOR INSPIRATION:
"The terrible thing about terrorism is that ultimately it destroys those who practice it. Slowly but surely, as they try to extinguish life in others, the light within them dies."   *Terry Waite (b. 1939)*
                              British religious adviser, hostage in Lebanon

"It seems to me a certainty that the fatalistic teachings of Mohammed and the utter degradation of the Arab women are the outstanding causes for the arrested development of the Arab. He is exactly as he was around the year 700, while we have been developing."   *General George S. Patton*

"If you are a terror to many, then beware of many."   *Ausonius*

"A man can't be too careful in the choice of his enemies."   *Oscar Wilde*

"(We've increased) the amount of warrior-type training we're putting into the schoolhouse ... (in) a program called Warrior Ethos. Warrior Ethos basically is that we're Soldiers first, that we'll never quit, mission will always come first, we refuse to accept defeat, and we'll never leave an American behind. Several years ago we developed the Army Values, seven values: loyalty, duty, respect, selfless service, honor, integrity and personal courage."   *Gen. Kevin P. Byrnes*

"Wilt thou draw near the nature of the Gods?
Draw near them then in being merciful, Sweet mercy is nobility's true badge."

William Shakespeare

"True nobility is exempt from fear." *Marcus Tullius Cicero*

"Put more trust in nobility of character than in an oath." *Solon*

REFLECTION: NOBILITY

A noble man is one that shows greatness in character and heart. A noble man is *uncompromising* in the maintenance of his purity both in his moral and social virtues. Nobility is the sum of all other virtues. It is a synthesis of courage, integrity, humility, prudence and fidelity. As the word "body" implies all the organs contained in a body, so the word "nobility" implies the sum of all other virtues. Nobility knows what is right and has the courage to stand up for what is noble and good. Wherever there is evil, a noble man feels called to act. He senses a stewardship that cannot allow evil to spoil that which is good. Noble men are men of resolution, compassion, faithfulness, and courage.

STUDY AND MEDITATION: NUMBERS 10:33-35

"So they set out from the mount of the LORD three days' journey. And the ark of the covenant of the LORD went before them three days' journey, to seek out a resting place for them. And the cloud of the LORD was over them by day, whenever they set out from the camp. And whenever the ark set out, Moses said, "Arise, O LORD, and let your enemies be scattered, and let those who hate you flee before you."

Through all of their journeys, the Lord was with the Israelites. The Ark contained the tablets of the law reminding people of the basis of God's covenant faithfulness to them and they carried it with them wherever they went. It is so closely associated with God that it is called the Ark of God thirty four times in the Old Testament. It is often mentioned in association with God's power and glory.

Not only did they have the Ark to remind them of God's faithfulness and power, but they had a cloud with them as they journeyed on to inspire them with confidence against their enemies. In our present struggle against evil, it is the same confidence in the faithfulness, power and glory of God that will give us victory over evil. Ephesians 6:11-12 teaches us that there are forces of evil at work in the world that are enemies of God's people. These are ultimately not flesh and blood but spiritual forces of evil that we war against. Our unshakable confidence in God and our unwavering commitment to struggle against evil spurs us on in the conflicts ahead.

DOCTRINE: R.L. DABNEY'S SYSTEMATIC THEOLOGY

XXIV.5 , "It is evidently the design of the Scriptures to make much of Satan and his work. From first to last, the favorite representation of the world's history is, that it is the arena for a struggle between two kingdoms – Christ's and Satan's. Christ leads the kingdom of the good, Satan that of the evil; though with different authorities and powers... His dominion is compacted by fear and hatred of God, and common purposes of malice. It is by their concert of action that they seem to approach so near to ubiquity in their influences. That Satan is also the tyrant and head of sinful men is equally plain. Satan originated sin and remains the leader of the human and angelic hosts which he seduced into hostility, and employs them in desperate resistance to Christ and His Father."

[20]

Question: **What does it mean when those serving with you are so willing and positive about their purpose in this war?**
Answer:

1. *It is an Argument that God has raised His servants to do some great work (Psalm 149:5-9).*
2. *It is an Argument that God will prosper those whom He has made so willing, (Judges 5:2).*
3. *It is an Argument that those who are so willing and positive about their purpose in this war, will go on courageously.*
4. *It is an Argument that they are so sure of the right and good nature of their Cause, that they will live and die for it.*

THOUGHTS FOR INSPIRATION:

"We are not 'born again' into soft and protected nurseries, but in the open country where we suck strength from the very terror of the tempest. 'We must through much tribulation enter into the kingdom of God.'"

Dr. J. H. Jowett

"If a man hasn't discovered something that he will die for, he isn't fit to live."

Martin Luther King, Jr.
June 23, 1963, Speech in Detroit

"It is impossible to win the race unless you venture to run, impossible to win the victory unless you dare to battle." *Richard M. DeVos*

"The will of God will never take you to where the grace of God will not protect you. To gain that which is worth having, it may be necessary to lose everything else." *Bernadette Devlin*

"That which I have preached I will seal with my blood!"
Last Words of a Christian Martyr, Rogers

"Thou threatenest me with Fire which burns for an hour, and so is extinguished; but knowest not the Fire of the Future Judgment, and of that Eternal Punishment, which is reserved for the Ungodly. But why tarriest thou? Bring forth what thou wilt!" *The Christian Martyr Polycarp*

"Self-confidence is either a petty pride in our own narrowness, or the realization of our duty and privilege as God's children." *Phillips Brooks*

"Jesus feels for thee; Jesus consoles thee; Jesus will help thee. No monarch in his impregnable fortress is more secure than the cony in his rocky burrow. The master of ten thousand chariots is not one whit better protected than the little dweller in the mountain's cleft. In Jesus the weak are strong, and the defenseless safe; they could not be more strong if they were giants, or more safe if they were in heaven. Faith gives to men on earth the protection of the God of heaven. More they cannot need, and need not wish. The conies cannot build a castle, but they avail themselves of what is there already: I cannot make myself a refuge, but Jesus has provided it, His Father has given it, His Spirit has revealed it, and lo, again tonight I enter it, and am safe from every foe." *Charles Haddon Spurgeon*

"Shadrach, Meshach, and Abednego answered and said to the king, 'O Nebuchadnezzar, we have no need to answer you in this matter. If this be so, our God whom we serve is able to deliver us from the burning fiery furnace, and he will deliver us out of your hand, O king. But if not, be it known to you, O king, that we will not serve your gods or worship the golden image that you have set up.'" Daniel 3:16-18

REFLECTION: RESOLUTION

"The man who will not execute his resolutions when they are fresh upon him can have no hope from them afterwards; they will be dissipated, lost and perish in the hurry and scurry of the world, or sunk in the slough of indolence."

Marie Edgeworth

Resolution is essentially a state of cognitive rest; a psychological state that exists when a man decides what he accepts as truth. There is no more questioning or indecision. For all the talk of *"open mindedness"*, the only place of psychological peace of mind is the state of *"closed mindedness"*. When a decision is made, the mind moves on to other things and peace is found.

A soldier must be resolute in his calling. He must have a firm hold on his convictions if he is to persevere in a time of war. The time for decision has past. The decision is made and the conflict is at hand. A man cannot act and reconsider at the same time. Resolution is indispensable for men at war. *"Resolution"* means that a soldier has answered the vital question, *"What is worth dying for?"*

STUDY AND MEDITATION: PSALM 149:5-9

"Let the godly exult in glory; let them sing for joy on their beds. Let the high praises of God be in their throats and two-edged swords in their hands, to execute vengeance on the nations and punishments on the peoples, to bind their kings with chains and their nobles with fetters of iron, to execute on them the judgment written! This is honor for all his godly ones. Praise the LORD!"

Psalm 149 is a song of confidence in the retribution of God against the enemies of His people. It remembers how Israel was charged with destroying God's enemies when they came into the Promised Land and it looks forward to that ultimate judgment when all the enemies of God will be destroyed in His righteous judgment. The double edged sword of the Christian is the *Word of God*. It is that Word that destroys all arguments and every proud obstacle to truth that man has contrived. It is that Word that brings light into the darkness that evil men love to dwell in. It is that Word that pierces the soul of man and shows him his guilt. It is that Word which will ultimately give God's people their victory over evil. It is that Word which is the mind of God, was manifested in the incarnation of the Messiah, and that goes out in our time with the power of the living Spirit of God, a power that cannot fail (2 Timothy 3:16).

DOCTRINE: WESTMINSTER CONFESSION OF FAITH

I.4, The authority of the Holy Scripture, for which it ought to be believed, and obeyed, dependeth not upon the testimony of any man, or Church; but wholly upon God (who is truth itself) the author thereof: and therefore it is to be received, because it is the Word of God.

[21]

Question: **What do you conclude from the good success that your side has already had?**
Answer:
1. *That Almighty God has declared Himself allied to our cause.*
2. *That he has already discouraged our enemies.*
3. *That we have every reason in the world to trust God for the future, who has done so much for us.*
4. *That the Lord will glorify Himself more and more for the sake of the Gospel.*

THOUGHTS FOR INSPIRATION:

"Victory belongs to the most persevering." *Napoleon*

"Never give up, never give in, and when the upper hand is ours, may we have the ability to handle the win with the dignity that we absorbed the loss."
Doug Williams

"No one can defeat us unless we first defeat ourselves." *Dwight Eisenhower*

"May God have mercy on my enemies because I won't"
General George S. Patton

"We cannot but acknowledge that God hath graciously patronized our cause and taken us under his special care, as he did his ancient covenant people."
Samuel Langdon, 1788

"I shall need...the favor of that Being in whose hands we are, who led our fathers, as Israel of old, from their native land and planted them in a country flowing with all the necessities and comforts of life." *Thomas Jefferson*

REFLECTION: ENCOURAGEMENT

A man that possesses the virtue of encouragement is one that reflects the good hopes and good possibilities to others and spurs them on to action. Enough with the prophets of doom and gloom! God has been good to those who have sought to do His will and walk in the paths of righteousness. We all need more people who will take note of the successes of God's people and encourage them to keep on both in walking on the paths of righteousness and in pursuing the cause God has set before them. Encouragement calls up hope, courage, and industry in others to help them to do all that God has called them to accomplish.

STUDY AND MEDITATION: EXODUS 17:8-13

"Then Amalek came and fought with Israel at Rephidim. So Moses said to Joshua, "Choose for us men, and go out and fight with Amalek. Tomorrow I will stand on the top of the hill with the staff of God in my hand." So Joshua did as Moses told him, and fought with Amalek, while Moses, Aaron, and Hur went up to the top of the hill. Whenever Moses held up his hand, Israel prevailed, and whenever he lowered his hand, Amalek prevailed. But Moses' hands grew weary, so they took a stone and put it under him, and he sat on it, while Aaron and Hur held up his hands, one on one side, and the other on the other side. So his hands were steady until the going down of the sun. And Joshua overwhelmed Amalek and his people with the sword."

Exodus 17 describes a nation of nomadic and warlike people called Amalekites descended from Amalek, the grandson of Esau. The Jewish historian Josephus tells us that Amalek was among the six grandsons of Esau by Aliphaz and that "These dwelt in that part of Idumea called Gebalitis, and in that denominated from Amalek, *Amalekites" &C Antiq.* ii.1. In describing the attack of the Amalekites on Moses, he specifies their country as "Goblitis and Petra" (iii. 2). These people arrayed themselves in opposition to the progress of God's people. God had given the people a charge to enter and possess the Promised Land. To avoid the conflict before them would pit them against God. There was no way to peace with God except through the Amalekites. They were weary and lacked the resources to carry out the battle. But God faithfully sustained His people and accomplished His will as they acted in concert and with valor.

God had already shown His ability to take care of His people by providing water from a spring bursting forth from a rock. Now, in the face of an attacking enemy, the Lord once again shows His miraculous care for His people by giving them victory. This power of God in their victory cannot be confused with their own ability however. God calls His people to obedience and faithfulness in the world. While God is in control of world affairs and the events of our lives, God calls us to act faithfully in response to those events. So the life to which we are called is a synthesis of obedience to duty coupled with enduring trust in the sovereign God.

DOCTRINE: WESTMINISTER CONFESSION OF FAITH

III.1, God from all eternity, did, by the most wise and holy counsel of His own will, freely, and unchangeably ordain whatsoever comes to pass: yet so, as thereby neither is God the author of sin, nor is violence offered to the will of the creatures; nor is the liberty or contingency of second causes taken away, but rather established.

[22]

Question: **What encouragement do you have from the support of our allies?**
Answer:
1. *We have cause to acknowledge God's great mercy, in bringing them to assist us in our cause.*
2. *Their numbers and preparations are impressive, and they are courageous in the face of evil.*
3. *They have given us enough assurance of their allegiance to our nation and to our cause.*
4. *They are as much concerned with the destruction of evil as we are, and they are resolved to join with us against this common threat to our Liberty.*

THOUGHTS FOR INSPIRATION:

"It isn't until you begin to fight in your own cause that you: *(a)* become really committed to winning, and; *(b)* become a genuine ally of other people struggling for their freedom." *Robin Morgan*

"A man of many companions may come to ruin,
  but there is a friend who sticks closer than a brother." *Proverbs 18:24*

"We cannot let terrorists hold this nation hostage or hold our allies hostage." *President George W. Bush*

"Geography has made us neighbors. History has made us friends. Economics has made us partners, and necessity has made us allies. Those whom God has so joined together, let no man put asunder." *President John F. Kennedy*

"Neutral men are the devil's allies."   *Edwin Hubbel Chapin*

"The darkest places in hell are reserved for those who remain neutral in times of moral crisis."   *Dante*

"Never doubt that a small group of thoughtful citizens can change the world. Indeed, it is the only thing that ever has."   *Margaret Mead*

REFLECTION: CONFIDENCE

Confidence is a state of mind that reflects an inner conviction and an expectation of success. Confidence based on a man's own ability may rise and fall with the events of the day but confidence based on the power and fidelity of God will sustain a man to complete any task the Lord places before him. Often the Lord confirms a man's confidence as He calls to his aid others of like mind and cause. The allies that gather against the storm of evil serve to reassure one another that they are not alone in this cause.

Ultimately our peace must come from a confidence in God and a commitment to live virtuously and righteously rather than a confidence in short-lived material achievements.

STUDY AND MEDITATION: ISAIAH 13:2-5

"On a bare hill raise a signal; cry aloud to them; wave the hand for them to enter the gates of the nobles. I myself have commanded my consecrated ones, and have summoned my mighty men to execute my anger, my proudly exulting ones. The sound of a tumult is on the mountains as of a great multitude! The sound of an uproar of kingdoms, of nations gathering together! The LORD of hosts is mustering a host for battle. They come from a distant land, from the end of the heavens, the LORD and the weapons of his indignation, to destroy the whole land."

In Isaiah 13, as the enemies of Israel had begun to gather in mass against the people of God, a loud call went out from God Himself to gather His own allies in the war against Evil. Battles that are waged for the cause of righteousness and justice are battles pitting good against evil. These battles have been waged since the beginning of time and will be waged until God has vanquished evil forever.

On the top of a bare mountain with maximum visibility, the forces of good are gathered. There the standard is raised where all men in the cause of freedom can gather. The standard is a call to those who are far off to join the cause of the common good. No matter how great the gains of the forces of evil, when God moves to destroy them, no army will stand against the infinite Creator, no matter how great they appear in the finite eyes of men.

DOCTRINE: WESTMINSTER CONFESSION OF FAITH
XXVI.1, All saints, that are united to Jesus Christ their Head, by His Spirit, and by faith, have fellowship with Him in His grace, sufferings, death, resurrection, and glory; they have communion in each other's gifts and graces, and are obliged to the performance of such duties, public and private, as do conduce to their mutual good, both in the inward and outward man.

[23]

Question: **Isn't it lamentable, that Christians professing a common citizenship in the Kingdom of God should find on their hands the blood of their brothers in Christ?**
Answer:
1. *I confess it is tragic: but as the situation now stands, there is an inevitable and absolute necessity of fighting laid upon the people of God in this cause.*
2. *God now calls upon us to avenge the blood of His Saints which has been shed, and those other outrageous acts of terror and war which have been committed against His people.*
3. *The whole Church of God calls upon us to come in to the help of the Lord and his people against this mighty evil spreading across the lands.*
4. *Our children and posterity call upon us to maintain those Liberties, and that Gospel, which we received from our fore-fathers.*
5. *We are not now to look at our enemies as brothers or Saints, but as the enemies of God, and our Faith, and allies of the Antichrist; and so our eye is not to pity them, nor our sword to spare them as Jeremiah said (48:10), "Cursed is he who does the work of the LORD with slackness, and cursed is he who keeps back his sword from bloodshed."*

INSPIRATIONAL THOUGHTS:
"I will never forget that I am an American, fighting for freedom, responsible for my actions, and dedicated to the principles which made my country free. I will trust in my God and in the United States of America."
                                        U.S. Armed Forces code of Conduct, Article VI

"The whole history of the progress of human liberty shows that all concessions yet made to her august claims have been born of earnest struggle. *If there is no struggle, there is no progress.* Those who profess to favor freedom, and yet deprecate agitation, are men who want crops without plowing up the ground, they want rain without thunder and lightning. They want the ocean without the awful roar of its many waters."

Frederick Douglass (1818-1895)

"A man can be free even within prison walls. Freedom is something spiritual. Whoever has once had it, can never lose it. There are some people who are never free outside a prison."

Unknown

"Do not take thought for your persons or your properties, but first and chiefly to care about the greatest improvement of the soul. I tell you that virtue is not given by money, but that from virtue come money and every other good of man, public as well as private... The difficulty, my friends, is not in avoiding death, but in avoiding unrighteousness; for that runs faster than death."

Socrates

"Noble souls, through dust and heat, rise from disaster and defeat the stronger."

Henry Wadsworth Longfellow

"Freedom is not an unlimited license, an unlimited choice, or an unlimited opportunity. Freedom is first of all a responsibility before the God from whom we come."

Alan Keyes

"I have often asked myself why human beings have any rights at all. I always come to the conclusion that human rights, human freedoms, and human dignity have their deepest roots somewhere outside the perceptible world. These values are as powerful as they are because, under certain circumstances, people accept them without compulsion and are willing to die for them."

Vaclav Havel

REFLECTION: JUSTICE

"To be perfectly just is an attribute of the divine nature; to be so to the utmost of our abilities, is the glory of man." Joseph Addison

It is puzzling how people that share a citizenship in the Kingdom of God can seek to destroy each other in the short time allotted to this life. Remarkably, we find that there are those who profess a faith like our own yet they serve a different master. All we can hope for is that our vision is clear and our cause is just. God and God alone will be the judge of a man's soul. If a man is to die in the midst of rebellion, we can only trust God's perfect judgment. Our compassion for an errant brother cannot dissuade us from the greater good of preserving life and liberty in our cause. No matter what a man's profession in speech, if his actions have made him an enemy of God then he is an enemy of mine.

STUDY AND MEDITATION: JOSHUA 7:19-22,25,26

"Then Joshua said to Achan, "My son, give glory to the LORD God of Israel and give praise to him. And tell me now what you have done; do not hide it from me." [20]And Achan answered Joshua, "Truly I have sinned against the LORD God of Israel, and this is what I did: [21]when I saw among the spoil a beautiful cloak from Shinar, and 200 shekels of silver, and a bar of gold weighing 50 shekels, then I coveted them and took them. And see, they are hidden in the earth inside my tent, with the silver underneath." [22]So Joshua sent messengers, and they ran to the tent; and behold, it was hidden in his tent with the silver underneath. And Joshua said, "Why did you bring trouble on us? The LORD brings trouble on you today." And all Israel stoned him with stones. They burned them with fire and stoned them with stones. [26]And they raised over him a great heap of stones that remains to this day. Then the LORD turned from his burning anger. Therefore, to this day the name of that place is called the Valley of Achor."

In Joshua 7, God had given specific instructions that no plunder was to be taken from the defeated armies falling before the people of Israel. Achan saw some pieces of silver and some gold and decided to increase his own *personal portfolio*. God wanted faithfulness and obedience from a pure and committed people. Achan risked the progress and success of God's people by rebelling and seeking his own progress independent of the good of all the other people. Achan's personal infidelity introduced sin and rebellion against God into the camp. The destruction of Achan included all of his family and servants. This was to blot out his name from any future generations. The judgment of God against this offender was carried out by those who knew him. This most difficult task had to be completed and it required an uncompromising vision for and an absolute commitment to the purposes of God.

DOCTRINE: CANONS OF DORT

Head II, Article 1, God is not only supremely merciful, but also supremely just. And his justice requires (as He hath revealed himself in his Word), that our sins committed against his infinite majesty should be punished, not only with temporal, but with eternal punishment, both in body and soul; which we cannot escape unless satisfaction be made to the justice of God.

[24]

Question: **There are a great many among our enemies that are considered to be honest men, will you make no distinction between them and others in combat?**
Answer:
1. *If they join themselves with the malignancy of our enemies, we cannot distinguish them from the malignants.*
2. *It has to be confessed, that they were never of us because they have aligned themselves with those who are cruel and evil and when their hypocrisy is exposed, they will prove to be the most dangerous enemies of all.*

THOUGHTS FOR CONSIDERATION:

"As hypocrisy is said to be the highest compliment to virtue, the art of lying is the strongest acknowledgment of the force of truth"   *William Hazlitt*

"A hypocrite is in himself both the archer and the mark, in all actions shooting at his own praise or profit."   *Thomas Fuller (1),*
Holy and Profane States—The Hypocrite   (maxim I, bk. V, ch. VIII)

"Hypocrisy is the homage which vice renders to virtue."
Francois Duc de la Rochefoucauld, Maximes (218)

"Not he who scorns the Savior's yoke should wear his cross upon the heart."
Johann Christoph Friedrich von Schiller,
The Fight with the Dragon (st. 24)

"Away, and mock the time with fairest show; False face must hide what the false heart doth know." *William Shakespeare, Macbeth (Macbeth act I, vii)*

"How inexpressible is the meanness of being a hypocrite! How horrible is it to be a mischievous and malignant hypocrite."   *Voltaire*

"For neither man nor angel can discern Hypocrisy, the only evil that walks Invisible, except to God alone, By his permissive will, through heav'n and earth."   *John Milton, Paradise Lost (bk. III, l. 682)*

"The true hypocrite is the one who ceases to perceive his deception, the one who lies with sincerity."   *André Gide*

REFLECTION: FIDELITY

In this case, fidelity is seen by it's opposite. No one who claims to love Christ can serve him and oppose Him at the same time. This is more than hypocrisy, it is infidelity. Fidelity is a commitment to what we have learned to be true. Infidelity is not simply a mistake or indifference but a deliberate disregard for the truth taught in the past. Those who are apathetic to the struggle against evil are not indifferent, they have rejected truth and are guilty of infidelity.

STUDY AND MEDITATION: MATTHEW 23:13-15

"But woe to you, scribes and Pharisees, hypocrites! For you shut the kingdom of heaven in people's faces. For you neither enter yourselves nor allow those who would enter to go in. Woe to you, scribes and Pharisees, hypocrites! For you travel across sea and land to make a single proselyte, and when he becomes a proselyte, you make him twice as much a child of hell as yourselves."

Matthew records Jesus scathing condemnation of those who shut up heaven from others by their lying and self-serving hypocrisy. The scribes and Pharisees would offer prayers for the poor and the widows making them think they were lifted up and approved by God but all the while, their suppression of truth kept the people from the knowledge of salvation. Is it any different when people give their money to the poor, travel great distances for their religion, faithfully pray throughout the day, and yet, every one they convert is twice as destined to Hell as they are. Hypocrisy is action without foundation. Hypocrisy is appearance without substance. Practice without truth is like a fork without food. No amount of appearance will make one justified before a holy God. John Calvin says, *"For this reason Isaiah derides the preposterous attempts of hypocrites, who zealously aimed at an external repentance by the observance of ceremony, but in the meanwhile cared not 'to loose the bands of wickedness, to undo the heavy burdens, and to let the oppressed go free'."*

DOCTRINE: INSTITUTES OF THE CHRISTIAN RELIGION

III.3.7, "Repentance proceeds from a sincere fear of God. Before the mind of the sinner can be inclined to repentance, he must be aroused by the thought of divine judgment; but when once the thought that God will one day ascend his tribunal and take an account of all words and actions has taken possession of his mind, it will not allow him to rest, or have one moment's peace, but will perpetually urge him to adopt a different plan of life, that he may be able to stand securely at that judgment-seat. Hence the Scripture, when exhorting to repentance, often introduces the subject of judgment as in Jeremiah, 'Lest my fury come forth like fire, and burn that none can quench it, because of the evil of your doings' *(Jeremiah 4:4)."*

[25]

Question: **Who do you believe are the Authors and instigators of this unnatural war?**
Answer:

1.   *This war was begun by those who oppose the Gospel of Jesus Christ.*
2.   *This war was begun by those who despise the Liberty of man and seek to preserve some control over ignorant masses.*
3.   *This war was begun by those desiring slavish control over free thinking people.*
4.   *This war was begun to disrupt peaceful societies and cause social turmoil and political destabilization in those societies.*
5.   *This war has made liberal use of covert actions, parasitic invasions, political manipulation, and sudden violence to expand and protract the conflict in obedience to teaching of the Qu'ran,*

> *"So when the sacred months have passed away, then slay the idolaters wherever you find them, and take them captive and besiege them and lie in wait for them in every ambush, then if they repent and keep up prayer and pay the poor-rate, leave their way free to them; surely Allah is Forgiving, Merciful" [Sura 9.5].*

> *"Those who reject Islam must be killed. If they turn back (from Islam), take (hold of) them and kill them wherever you find them....: Surah 8:67, The Noble Qu'ran*

> *"It is not for a Prophet that he should have prisoners of war (and free them with ransom) until he had made a great slaughter (among his enemies) in the land." Surah 8:67, The Noble Qu'ran*

> *"And fight them until there is no more Ritnah (disbelief and polytheism, i.e., worshipping others besides Allah) and the religion (worship) will all be for Allah Alone [in the whole of the world]. But if they cease (worshipping others besides Allah), then certainly, Allah is All-Seer of what they do." Surah 8:39, The Noble Qu'ran*

THOUGHTS FOR INSPIRATION:

"The world must be made safe for democracy."   *Woodrow T. Wilson*
(28th president of the United States 1856-1924)

"The terrorists were at war with us, but we were not yet at war with them. For more than 20 years, the terrorist threat gathered, and America's response across several administrations of both parties was insufficient. Historically, democratic societies have been slow to react to gathering threats, tending instead to wait to confront threats until they are too dangerous to ignore or until it is too late."   *Dr. Condoleezza Rice*
As *National Security Advisor*

"It is also a reminder of the great purpose of our great land, and that is to rid this world of evil and terror. The evil ones have roused a mighty nation, a mighty land. And for however long it takes, I am determined that we will prevail."   *President George W. Bush*

"In a second world war, we learned there is no isolation from evil. We affirmed that some crimes are so terrible they offend humanity, itself. And we resolved that the aggressions and ambitions of the wicked must be opposed early, decisively, and collectively, before they threaten us all. That evil has returned, and that cause is renewed."   *President George W. Bush*

"Given the means, our enemies would be a threat to every nation and, eventually, to civilization itself. So we're determined to fight this evil, and fight until we're rid of it. We will not wait for the authors of mass murder to gain the weapons of mass destruction. We act now, because we must lift this dark threat from our age and save generations to come."   *President George W. Bush*

REFLECTION: CONVICTION

"Never, 'for the sake of peace and quiet,' deny your own experience or convictions" *Dag Hammarskjold*

In the days of struggle we are apt to find ourselves in, it will be only our convictions that what we struggle for is true and what we war against is evil. If we falter in that simple conviction, we will *"blink"* and give our enemy an opportunity to destroy us. It is becoming our duty to remain steadfast in our convictions despite those with small voices and large platforms who seek to convince us otherwise. Test your own convictions to see if they are good, honest, and worthy. If they are all of those things, then you will outlast any enemy that serves a lesser conviction than your own.

STUDY AND MEDITATION: ISAIAH 61:1

"The Spirit of the Lord GOD is upon me, because the LORD has anointed me to bring good news to the poor; he has sent me to bind up the brokenhearted, to proclaim liberty to the captives, and the opening of the prison to those who are bound."

Many have called *"The Spirit of the Lord"*, God's Tempest! Rather than falling like a gentle dew in the morning, He comes like a stormy wind over raging waters. This Spirit of the Lord comes to powerfully proclaim God's Word and His plan for Man. This powerful proclamation let's us know that this is from God Himself.

In Isaiah 61, the Spirit teaches that God has anointed Israel to proclaim and bring His Good News to all people who will receive it. God will mercifully minister to the brokenhearted, He will authoritatively proclaim liberty to those held hostage to fear, oppression and death, and He will set free those who are bound by oppression and sin.

From Israel came the Messiah, Jesus Christ who proclaimed this very message and accomplished it on the cross. That was not the end, it was only the beginning. Now the church continues the proclamation of the Good News as the body of Christ until He returns.

DOCTRINE: INSTITUTES OF CHRISTIAN RELIGION

Book I, Chapter V, It is impossible to doubt the punishment of crimes; while at the same time he, in no unequivocal manner, declares that he is the protector, and even the avenger of innocence, by shedding blessings on the good, helping their necessities, soothing and solacing their griefs, relieving their sufferings, and in all ways providing for their safety. And though he often permits the guilty to exult for a time with impunity, and the innocent to be driven to and fro in adversity, nay, even to be wickedly and iniquitously oppressed, this ought not to produce any uncertainty as to the uniform justice of all his procedure.

[26]

Question: **Do not many of them that you count your enemies, stand for "Religion" as well as you?**

ANSWER:

1. *Yes, and some it would seem do better than we do; for we often pretend it, and they intend it but only in madness. Who but mad men can think that Terrorists will fight in defense of religious liberty and freedom.*

2. *Neither is it to be imagined, that men so loose, lewd, and wicked, as most of the Jihadists, terrorists, and extremists are, should really intend the preservation of religious liberty or any thing else that is good.*
3. *We know that murderous villains such as Osama bin Laden and Abu-Musab al-Zarqawi pretend to fight for Religion, yet they commit every form of atrocity known to man in their religious zeal. Rather than preserving religion, they risk everything religion teaches to advance themselves.*
4. *Our outrage and pursuit of those whom the world acknowledged as zealots sufficiently shows how we actually stand for true religious fidelity.*
5. *Our foes stand for religion just as the Ephesians stood for Diana, in Acts 19.*
   a. *They stand for false prophets*
   b. *They stand for ignominious clergy*
   c. *They stand for soul-starving Scriptures*
   d. *They stand for a litany of empty religious ceremonies*
   e. *They stand against religious liberty*
   f. *They stand against individual conscience*

THOUGHTS FOR CONSIDERATION:

"Various kinds of ideas can be classified by their relationship to the authentication process. There are ideas systematically prepared for authentication ("theories"), ideas not derived from any systematic process ("visions"), ideas which could not survive any reasonable authentication process ("illusions"), ideas which exempt themselves from any authentication process ("myths"), ideas which have already passed authentication processes ("facts"), as well as ideas known to have failed—or certain to fail—such processes ("falsehoods"—both mistakes and lies)."   *Thomas Sowell*

"If there were a verb meaning 'to believe falsely,' it would not have any significant first person, present indicative."   *Ludwig Wittgenstein*

"I always divide people into two groups. Those who live by what they know to be a lie, and those who live by what they believe, falsely, to be the truth."
                                        Christopher Hampton

"Falsehood is often rocked by truth, but she soon outgrows her cradle, and discards her nurse."   *George Colman, "The Younger"*

"Better suffer for truth, than prosper by falsehood."   *Danish Proverb*

"Religion must be taught, not forced."   *Latin Proverb*

REFLECTION: NOBILITY

It is not enough to profess some form of religion or religious virtue. That religion must be able to demonstrate consistency with the character of God evidenced everywhere and particularly in the Christian Scriptures. Men so convinced of the truth and veracity of those same Scriptures are then compelled to act in obedience to them. There is a perfect harmony between the Christian faith as it is taught in the Scriptures and the rest of creation. All that is noble and good is taught to man by God there. Examining the Commandments from Exodus or the Beatitudes in Matthew demonstrates the order and the grace of the Christian faith. Men of nobility strive to avoid any form of hypocrisy by giving full expression to the doctrines of Christianity. That testimony will shame our enemy and encourage our friends.

STUDY AND MEDITATION: ACTS 17:22-31

"So Paul, standing in the midst of the Areopagus, said: "Men of Athens, I perceive that in every way you are very religious. For as I passed along and observed the objects of your worship, I found also an altar with this inscription, 'To the unknown god.' What therefore you worship as unknown, this I proclaim to you. The God who made the world and everything in it, being Lord of heaven and earth, does not live in temples made by man, nor is he served by human hands, as though he needed anything, since he himself gives to all mankind life and breath and everything. And he made from one man every nation of mankind to live on all the face of the earth, having determined allotted periods and the boundaries of their dwelling place, that they should seek God, in the hope that they might feel their way toward him and find him. Yet he is actually not far from each one of us, for" 'In him we live and move and have our being' as even some of your own poets have said, "'For we are indeed his offspring.' Being then God's offspring, we ought not to think that the divine being is like gold or silver or stone, an image formed by the art and imagination of man. The times of ignorance God overlooked, but now he commands all people everywhere to repent, because he has fixed a day on which he will judge the world in righteousness by a man whom he has appointed; and of this he has given assurance to all by raising him from the dead."

In Acts 17, Paul stood in the middle of a large gathering of men who imagined themselves to be among the most religious men in the world. It was said that it was easier to find an idol in Athens than it was a man. So concerned were they that a god might be offended that they even created an altar to an unknown god. Paul respectfully acknowledges their religious devotion, however misguided it may have been. While respecting their religious zeal, Paul doesn't hesitate to speak the truth against all that they believe. He didn't do this to condemn, that will be done by God, rather, he did it out of compassion and obedience. Paul was compassionate towards the ignorant and misled and he was obedient to the command of Christ that he should be a vessel of righteousness carrying forth the good news that God has made a way to escape condemnation brought by religious speculation and superstition. Paul brings the Gospel of Peace and the knowledge of the true God to paranoid people striving to satisfy the religious requirements laid upon them by men. Rather than a religion crafted in the mind of men, Paul brings them something completely different and reveals to them that the one true God is where we all have our existence. God doesn't belong to any one government or nation but all peoples everywhere belong to Him. And, all peoples everywhere will be held accountable to their response to His revelation of truth which they have received.

DOCTRINE: BELGIC CONFESSION
Article 1, We believe with the heart, and confess with the mouth, that there is one only simple and spiritual Being, which we call God; and that He is eternal, incomprehensible, invisible, immutable, infinite, almighty, perfectly wise, just, good, and the overflowing fountain of all good.

[27]

Question: **Do you think that there will be a Reformation of these things, before we shall enjoy any peace?**
Answer: *Yes, there must be for these reasons.*
1. *Because a just God is not unconcerned with the plight of His people.*
2. *His anger is roused by unholy Covenants made in false religion and ungodly rebellions.*
3. *God is concerned for the just, the widows, the orphans, and the defenseless. Surely He has not turned His gaze away from the oppressed Arabs under the terrorist's control.*
4. *Because every Century or so the Church has undergone reformation.*
5. *Because the Devil and his Instruments have become so stirred up in this conflict, being let loose for a time.*
6. *Because the Church of Christ in all of Christendom prays for, and expects reformation.*
7. *Because the measure of our enemies' iniquities is becoming full.*

THOUGHTS FOR INSPIRATION:

"Let your religion be less of a theory and more of a love affair."

G.K. Chesterton

"The American Revolution was a beginning, not a consummation."

Woodrow Wilson

"You are a human being. You have rights inherent in that reality. You have dignity and worth that exists prior to law."　　　*Lyn Beth Neylon*

"Freedom has its life in the hearts, the actions, the spirit of men and so it must be daily earned and refreshed—else like a flower cut from its life-giving roots, it will wither and die."　　　*Dwight D. Eisenhower*

"This, then, is the state of the union: free and restless, growing and full of hope. So it was in the beginning. So it shall always be, while God is willing, and we are strong enough to keep the faith."　　　*Lyndon B. Johnson*

"I would remind you that extremism in the defense of liberty is no vice! And let me remind you also that moderation in the pursuit of justice is no virtue."

Barry Goldwater

"Give to every human being every right that you claim for yourself."

Robert Ingersoll

"It is easy to take liberty for granted, when you have never had it taken from you."　　　*Vice-President Richard (Dick) Cheney*

REFLECTION: PURITY

"To reform a world, to reform a nation, no wise man will undertake; and all but foolish men know that the only solid, though a far slower reformation, is what each begins and perfects on himself." *Thomas Carlyle*

Purity has become a flexible word with all but the proper connotations. When the word is used today, it is almost exclusively reserved for sexuality. It has other equally valuable uses. Purity in thought and conduct can mean that an individual possess a doctrine or view untainted by errors injected by other men. Certainly that is a purity we ought to strive for. Only by seeking a purity in our religious views and occupations can we see a reformation of religious thought. When men become concerned with pure doctrine rather than political innovations, the Church will see a reform of conviction that will alter the religious landscape far into the future.

STUDY AND MEDITATION: ISAIAH 29:18-24

"In that day the deaf shall hear the words of a book, and out of their gloom and darkness the eyes of the blind shall see. The meek shall obtain fresh joy in the LORD, and the poor among mankind shall exult in the Holy One of Israel.

For the ruthless shall come to nothing and the scoffer cease, and all who watch to do evil shall be cut off, who by a word make a man out to be an offender, and lay a snare for him who reproves in the gate, and with an empty plea turn aside him who is in the right.

Therefore thus says the LORD, who redeemed Abraham, concerning the house of Jacob: "Jacob shall no more be ashamed, no more shall his face grow pale. For when he sees his children, the work of my hands, in his midst, they will sanctify my name; they will sanctify the Holy One of Jacob and will stand in awe of the God of Israel. And those who go astray in spirit will come to understanding, and those who murmur will accept instruction."

Isaiah points out that despite God's command to trust only in Him and not call out to pagan nations for protection, the Assyrian shadow had fell upon Jerusalem and the temptation to call for Egyptian help was overwhelming. The king, Hezekiah, struggled to believe and wanted the security of an earthly ally. He had learned to rely upon man rather than God alone. He was not alone. The people of God had also turned away. They imagined that God didn't see their injustice and selfish actions. They wanted all the appearances of a pious people but their hearts had forgotten the way of grace. Now, the prophet Isaiah reminded the people that God had seen everything. He had seen and knew everything, including their hearts. The people learned that God is never ignored, He is either believed and followed or rebelled against. There is no neutrality. Thus, the people had actually been in rebellion against God in their selfish pursuits, they had plotted against God because they had not planned to live for Him.

Isaiah described the marks of a fallen and corrupt people of God and promised that things were going to change. He promised a new age and a time of rejoicing. Isaiah gave them a glimpse of a revived and pure people, a church, cleansed by the action of God. This work of God is in keeping with His promise to Abraham that anyone who is in Christ will receive the blessings God promised to Abraham. Their shame will be removed and they will be made a clean, virtuous, and redeemed people. God Himself will transform the world He created from one which the ruthless and evil doers have turned into gloom and darkness into one of peace and justice in which the humble will rejoice. This is the Messianic age.

DOCTRINE: WILLIAM G. T. SHEDD

"Sanctification though progressive is not complete in this life: 'If we say we have no sin, we deceive ourselves' (1 John 1:8,10); 'brethren, I count not myself to have apprehended, but I press toward the mark' (Philippians 3:12-14); 'I know that in me, that is in my flesh, dwells no good thing. I see another law in my members, warring against the law of my mind' (Romans 7:18, 23; Galatians 5:7). Sanctification is completed at death: 'The souls of believers at their death are made perfect in holiness' (Westminster Shorter Catechism Q. 37). The heavenly Jerusalem contains 'the spirits of just men made perfect' (Hebrews 12:23); 'we shall be like him, for we shall see him as he is' (1 John 3:2): 'absent from the body and present with the Lord' (2 Corinthians 5:8); 'Christ loved the church that he might sanctify it and present it to himself a glorious church not having spot or wrinkle' (Ephesians 5:27); 'now we see through a glass darkly; but when that which is perfect is come, face to face' (1 Corinthians 13:12); 'the pure in heart shall see God' (Matthew 5:8); 'blessed are the dead who die in the Lord' (Revelation 14:13). Sanctification once begun is never wholly lost. It fluctuates with the fidelity of the believer, but he never falls back into the stupor and death of the unregenerate state..."[8]

PART II

The Qualification of our Soldiers

[28]

Question: **What are the principal things required of a soldier?**
Answer:
1. *That he be religious and godly.*
2. *That he be courageous and valiant.*
3. *That he be skillful in the Military Profession.*

THOUGHTS FOR INSPIRIATION:

"A few honest men are better than numbers." *Oliver Cromwell*

"Build me a son, O Lord, who will be strong enough to know when he is weak, and brave enough to face himself when he is afraid, one who will be proud and unbending in honest defeat, and humble and gentle in victory."

General Douglas MacArthur

"The military virtues are: bravery in the soldier, courage in the officer, valor in the general, but guided by the principles or order and discipline, dominated by vigilance and foresight." *General Alexander Suvarov*

"The character of a soldier is high. They who stand forth the foremost in danger, for the community, have the respect of mankind. An officer is much more respected than any other man who has as little money. In a commercial country, money will always purchase respect. But you find, an officer, who has, properly speaking, no money, is every where well received and treated with attention. The character of a soldier always stands him in good stead."

Boswell: Life of Johnson

"Obedience to lawful authority is the foundation of manly character."

Robert E. Lee

"A noble man compares and estimates himself by an idea which is higher than himself; and a mean man, by one lower than himself. The one produces aspiration; the other ambition, which is the way in which a vulgar man aspires."

Marcus Aurelius

REFLECTION: RELIABILITY

Reliability is a virtue that is born of both competence and fidelity. It is a blend of the intellect and the will. A reliable person is one aware of his duties and able to carry them out. He also desires to carry them out and so, rather than doing what is required, he does what is necessary and perhaps even more. A reliable man is trusted to do his duty and keep the good faith of his superiors.

STUDY AND MEDITATION: 1 CHRONICLES 5:18-22

"The Reubenites, the Gadites, and the half-tribe of Manasseh had valiant men who carried shield and sword, and drew the bow, expert in war, 44,760, able to go to war. They waged war against the Hagrites, Jetur, Naphish, and Nodab. And when they prevailed over them, the Hagrites and all who were with them were given into their hands, for they cried out to God in the battle, and he granted their urgent plea because they trusted in him. They carried off their livestock: 50,000 of their camels, 250,000 sheep, 2,000 donkeys, and 100,000 men alive. For many fell, because the war was of God. And they lived in their place until the exile."

1 Chronicles 5 records the events in the war of the trans-Jordanic tribes of Israel with the Arabic tribes. The men are called valiant warriors. They were men carrying shields for defense and sword for the offence. There were others who drew the bow as skilful bowmen. They were trained in the art of war and executed their profession with expertise. The war described here was a serious conflict with significant consequences. The possession of the land was at stake. The procession of the land for the raising of livestock was such a serious matter that wars leading to extermination of the enemy was accepted as the norm. The enemy of God's people, though outnumbering the Israelites, fell in great numbers and suffered an horrendous defeat because this was a "war of God". The people called out to God and because of their sincerity of faith in Him, God delivered their enemies to them.

DOCTRINE: SECOND HELVETIC CONFESSION

XII.1, We teach that the will of God is set down unto us in the law of God, to wit, what He would have us to do, or not to do, what is good and just, or what is evil and unjust. We therefore confess that the law is holy,... and good" (Romans 7:12); and that this law is, by the finger of God, either written in the hearts of men (Romans 2:15), and so is called the law of nature, or engraven in the two tables of stone, and more largely expounded in the books of Moses (Exodus 20:1-17; Deuteronomy 5:22). For plainness' sake we divide it into the moral law, which is contained in the commandments, or the two tables expounded in the books of Moses; into the ceremonial, which does appoint ceremonies and the worship of God; and into the judicial law, which is occupied about political and domestic affairs.

[29]

Question: **How do you prove that a soldier should be religious?**
Answer:
1. *By Scripture,*
    Deuteronomy 23:9, "When you are encamped against your enemies, then you shall keep yourself from every evil thing."
    Luke 3:14, "Soldiers also asked him, 'And we, what shall we do?' And he said to them, 'Do not extort money from anyone by threats or by false accusation, and be content with your wages.'"
2. *Because soldiers must face death and be assured of their eternal destiny*
3. *Because soldiers stand in continual need of God's help.*
4. *Because every war is a religious war weighing heavy on the moral convictions of men.*
5. *Because the most courageous and virtuous armies of history have been armies of deep religious conviction.*
6. *Because a well ordered Army is a School of Virtue teaching the disciplines of:*
    a. *Loyalty*
    b. *Duty*
    c. *Responsibility*
    d. *Selfless-service*
    e. *Honor*
    f. *Integrity*
    g. *Personal Courage*
    h. *Respect*

THOUGHTS FOR INSPIRATION:
"I never had a policy; I have just tried to do my very best each and every day."   *Abraham Lincoln*

"I hate mankind, for I think myself one of the best of them, and I know how bad I am."   *Samuel Johnson*

"Love all, trust a few, do wrong to none."   *William Shakespeare*

"Character is doing the right thing when nobody's looking. There are too many people who think that the only thing that's right is to get by, and the only thing that's wrong is to get caught."   *J.C. Watts*

"If you have integrity, nothing else matters. If you don't have integrity, nothing else matters."   *Alan Simpson*

"Character is much easier kept than recovered."   *Thomas Paine*

"Selfishness is not living as one wishes to live, it is asking others to live as one wishes to live."   *Oscar Wilde,*
The Soul of Man Under Socialism

"I hope I shall possess firmness and virtue enough to maintain, what I consider the most enviable of all titles, the character of an 'honest man.' Your honesty influences others to be honest."   *George Washington*

REFLECTION: INTEGRITY
The root of the word integrity comes from the Latin meaning "wholeness". That is an apt description of a man of integrity, he is whole and undivided. He speaks with a single purpose and cannot be described as double-minded or two-faced. Good citizenship can pretend many virtues but integrity belongs to the inner man, it springs directly from the heart. Integrity cannot be pretended. People may be fooled but in fooling them, integrity has not actually been pretended, but dishonesty emerged as a character trait.

The first place integrity is exercised is with the self, then with God, and then the world. If either of the first two are neglected, the last will never be consistently tried.

THOUGHTS FOR STUDY AND MEDITATION: 1 PETER 1:13-19

"Therefore, preparing your minds for action, and being sober-minded, set your hope fully on the grace that will be brought to you at the revelation of Jesus Christ. As obedient children, do not be conformed to the passions of your former ignorance, but as he who called you is holy, you also be holy in all your conduct, since it is written, "You shall be holy, for I am holy." And if you call on him as Father who judges impartially according to each one's deeds, conduct yourselves with fear throughout the time of your exile, knowing that you were ransomed from the futile ways inherited from your forefathers, not with perishable things such as silver or gold, but with the precious blood of Christ, like that of a lamb without blemish or spot."

A Christian soldier's mind must be prepared and set for action. The language here makes us think of a runner with his feet in the starting blocks waiting for the sound to begin his sprint. Never knowing when the call will come, a soldier must always have his affairs in order and always conduct himself as if the hour he lives will be the hour of his testing. Thus, sober-mindedness or clear focus is necessary as a mental discipline for soldiers. There is no opportunity for a soldier's mind to wander. Virtuous character requires a vigilant mind. Finally, a soldier's hope when facing danger cannot be in the praise of the citizens or even on the competence of commanders or equipment but only on that finished work of Jesus Christ that grants a peace in the soul unknown by the wicked and unjust. While our enemy dies in fear, we are able to die in a sure confidence that we go on to something far better.

DOCTRINE: WESTMINSTER CONFESSION OF FAITH

XIX.5 The moral law doth forever bind all, as well justified persons as others, to the obedience thereof; and that, not only in regard of the matter contained in it, but also in respect of the authority of God the Creator, who gave it. Neither doth Christ, in the gospel, any way dissolve, but much strengthen this obligation.

[30]

Question: **Who are the chief offenders against this rule?**
Answer: *Those Soldiers that give themselves to Whoring and Uncleanness; not only privately by practice, but also publicly by theory, and supporting such causes that promote immoral and ungodly conduct.*

THOUGHTS FOR INSPIRATION:

"Do we think that when the day has been idly spent and squandered away by us, we shall be fit to work when the night and darkness come—when our understanding is weak, and our memory frail, and our will crooked, and by long custom of sinning obstinately bent the wrong way, what can we then do in religion? What reasonable or acceptable service can we then perform to God? When our candle is just sinking into the socket, how shall our light "so shine before men that they may see our good works"?... I will not pronounce anything concerning the impossibility of a death-bed repentance, but I am sure that it is very difficult, and, I believe, very rare." *John Tillotson*

"A sinning man will stop praying. A praying man will stop sinning."
Unknown

"If you are ever tempted to think that we modern Western Europeans cannot really be so very bad because we are, comparatively speaking, humane—if, in other words, you think God might be content with us on that ground—ask yourself whether you think God ought to have been content with the cruelty of past ages because they excelled in courage or chastity. You will see at once that this is an impossibility. From considering how the cruelty of our ancestors looks to us, you may get some inkling of how our softness, worldliness, and timidity would have looked to them, and hence how both must look to God." *C. S. Lewis*

"We know that unholy men, in order to gratify the flesh, anxiously lay hold on whatever is set forth in Scripture *respecting* the infinite goodness of God; and hypocrites also, as far as they can, maliciously darken the knowledge of it, as though the grace of God extinguished the desire for a godly life, and opened to audacity the door of sin." *John Calvin*
(Commentary on Romans 12:1)

"Get correct views of life, and learn to see the world in its true light. It will enable you to live pleasantly, to do good, and, when summoned away, to leave without regret." *Robert E. Lee*

REFLECTON: LUCIDITY

Lucidity is a transparency. It is clarity in thinking. It is honesty about the objective truths of life. Intellectual courage is a refusal to act on the basis of falsehood. It is easy to "go along with popular conventions" rather than to think thoroughly about the virtues and the axioms of life. It takes courage to come under conviction and live accordingly. The path of least resistance is found in following the mindless currents of popular behavior. Blending in and remaining a part of the anonymous collective gives a false peace that hides our loss of individuality. The risk of owning our convictions and deciding upon truth is called, "lucidity."

THOUGHTS FOR STUDY AND MEDIATION: ROMANS 12:1-2

"I appeal to you therefore, brothers, by the mercies of God, to present your bodies as a living sacrifice, holy and acceptable to God, which is your spiritual worship. Do not be conformed to this world, but be transformed by the renewal of your mind, that by testing you may discern what is the will of God, what is good and acceptable and perfect."

Paul is making an urgent appeal to his readers. Their motivations to follow after God's law have been diminished by their misunderstanding of forgiveness and grace. Knowing they can do nothing in the flesh to merit salvation, they have wrongly concluded that their conduct is outside of God's interest. Paul is telling them that they should consider their bodies as a living sacrifice. He means to give them a picture of complete dedication. A sacrifice is consumed in the offering and so they are to be consumed with a holy zeal for God in all areas of their life. He encourages them to not look like the world which is still lost in sin but to be transformed by their changed thinking. Thus, they are proving not in theory but in practice what is good, acceptable and perfect in the will of God. Not only will they be pleasing God but their lives become living testimonies of God's power to change a person from a vile offender to a victor in Christ.

DOCTRINE: WESTMINSTER CONFESSION OF FAITH

XI.5, God doth continue to forgive the sins of those that are justified; and, although they can never fall from the state of justification, yet they may, by their sins, fall under God's fatherly displeasure, and not have the light of His countenance restored unto them, until they humble themselves, confess their sins, beg pardon, and renew their faith and repentance.

[31]

Question: **Shouldn't Soldiers be expected to commit immoral acts in the profession of arms?**
Answer: *No more in the profession of arms than in any other profession. The Scriptures say to all men without distinction:*
   1.   *"God will judge the sexually immoral and adulterous" (Hebrews 13:4).*
   2.   *"The Lord will not hold him guiltless who takes his name in vain" (Ex. 20:7).*
   3.   *"Drunkards will not inherit the Kingdom of God" (1 Corinthians 6:10).*
   4.   *"The Wrongdoer will be paid back for the wrong he has done, and there is no partiality" (Colossians 3:25).*

THOUGHTS FOR INSPIRATION:

"I haven't, in the 23 years that I have been in the uniformed services of the United States of America, ever violated an order—not one."   *Oliver North*

"Punishment is now unfashionable... because it creates moral distinctions among men, which, to the democratic mind, are odious. We prefer a meaningless collective guilt to a meaningful individual responsibility."   *Thomas Szasz*

"Although the legal and ethical definitions of right are the antithesis of each other, most writers use them as synonyms. They confuse power with goodness, and mistake law for justice."   *Charles T. Sprading*

"The trouble with the laws these days is that criminals know their rights better than their wrongs."   *Author Unknown*

"No man suffers injustice without learning, vaguely but surely, what justice is."   *Isaac Rosenfeld*

"It was belief in a just, divine government of the world which made it possible to dispense with the perhaps effective but certainly un-Christian practices of killing the innocent-torture, extortion, and the rest. War now always remained a kind of appeal to the arbitration of God, which both sides were willing to accept. It is only when Christian faith is lost that man must himself make use of all means, even criminal ones, in order to secure by force the victory of his cause."   *Dietrich Bonheoffer, Ethics p.94*

REFLECTION: RESPECT

Our capacity to respect anyone will depend on our understanding of the nature of man. We tend to respect others when they respect us. The challenge comes when someone does not respect us and we are called to decide how we will view them in return.

The supreme example of "respect" (along with love and other virtues) is found in Christian history. As Jesus Christ hung from a cross, crucified according to Roman law, he looked at his accusers and executioners and asked God to forgive them because of their ignorance.

A view of man that aligns itself with truth, will accept that all men were created in the image of God. Even when justice requires war or execution, respect for the inherent dignity of mankind can still be held. War doesn't require hate. War doesn't require a low view of man. War can cost the victor his own soul if he succumbs to a subjective view of man.

THOUGHTS FOR STUDY AND MEDITATION: MICAH 6:8

"He has told you, O man, what is good; and what does the LORD require of you but to do justice, and to love kindness, and to walk humbly with your God?"

The Scriptures are clear that no form of religious observance can save the soul of any person. Instead, the purity of saving faith is evidenced in conduct. Namely, that conduct which embraces the Great Commandments of doing righteously and exercising love. These two duties of all Christians in every context both summarize the Law given in the Ten Commandments and also reflect the teaching of Christ that we must love God and our neighbor. The third principle in Micah is that we must walk humbly with God; that is, in fellowship with God. Recognizing his greatness as the prophet Isaiah did in Isaiah 6, we walk, or live, with the greatness and holiness of God always in view. We know that none of our conduct is ever outside of his view or concern, even in times of war. We acknowledge that no conflict is our own but that God is the arbiter of every conflict among men.

DOCTRINE: WESTMINSTER LARGER CATECHISM
Q. 140, *What are the duties required in the eighth commandment?*
The duties required in the eighth commandment are, truth, faithfulness, and justice in contracts and commerce between man and man; rendering to everyone his due, restitution of goods unlawfully detained from the right owners thereof, giving and lending freely, according to our abilities, and the necessities of others; moderation of our judgments, wills, and affections concerning worldly goods; a provident care and study to get, keep, use, and dispose these things which are necessary and convenient for the sustentation of our nature, and suitable to our condition; a lawful calling, and diligence in it; frugality; avoiding unnecessary lawsuits, and suretyship, or other like engagements; and an endeavor, by all just and lawful means, to procure, preserve, and further the wealth and outward estate of others, as well as our own.

[32]

Question: **Why are there so many lewd and wicked men in military service?**
Answer:
1. *Because all men can be considered wicked under the curse of original sin; only some have learned discipline and have surrendered to a higher calling and principled living.*
2. *Because Commanders have not been offered a moral criteria for selecting officers.*
3. *Because honest and religious men shrink back from the pagan environment they often find themselves in when they serve in the military.*

4. *Because good order and discipline is not more strictly enforced by supervisors and officers.*
5. *Because volunteers are often seeking benefits for themselves rather than seeking to serve others selflessly.*

THOUGHTS FOR INSPIRATION:

"Responsibility: A detachable burden easily shifted to the shoulders of God, Fate, Fortune, Luck or one's neighbor. In the days of astrology it was customary to unload it upon a star."   *Ambrose Bierce,*
The Devil's Dictionary, 1911

"Few men have virtue to withstand the highest bidder." *George Washington*

"We have not passed that subtle line between childhood and adulthood until we have stopped saying, 'It got lost,' and say 'I lost it'."   *.Sidney J. Harris*

"This nation will remain the land of the free only so long as it is the home of the brave."   *Elmer Davis*

"Leadership is a potent combination of strategy and character. But if you must be without one, be without the strategy."   *Norman Schwarzkopf*

"In the beginning of a change, the patriot is a scarce man, and brave, and hated and scorned. When his cause succeeds, the timid join him, for then it costs nothing to be a patriot."   *Mark Twain, Notebook, 1935*

"The LORD saw that the wickedness of man was great in the earth, and that every intention of the thoughts of his heart was only evil continually."
Genesis 6:5

REFLECTION: SELFLESSNESS

This virtue often proves the most elusive because it can only be authenticated when the price to the one serving others is high. When service is rendered from one person to another, expressions of gratitude or a reputation as a person of good will are often the reward. True selflessness must be exercised without a reward however. It cannot be born out of a need for recognition or self authentication. It must spring from love and compassion. It must reflect a sense of duty to something higher than self. It must expect nothing in return and be happy simply to have served. Only when the conditions are such as they are in war, can true selflessness be demonstrated. It is often the last act of a soldier who gives his own life in defense of his friends. *"Greater love has no one than this, that someone lays down his life for his friends."* John 15:13

THOUGHTS FOR STUDY AND MEDITATION: MARK 14:66-72

"And as Peter was below in the courtyard, one of the servant girls of the high priest came, and seeing Peter warming himself, she looked at him and said, 'You also were with the Nazarene, Jesus.' But he denied it, saying, 'I neither know nor understand what you mean.' And he went out into the gateway and the rooster crowed. And the servant girl saw him and began again to say to the bystanders, 'This man is one of them.' But again he denied it. And after a little while the bystanders again said to Peter, 'Certainly you are one of them, for you are a Galilean.' But he began to invoke a curse on himself and to swear, 'I do not know this man of whom you speak.' And immediately the rooster crowed a second time. And Peter remembered how Jesus had said to him, 'Before the rooster crows twice, you will deny me three times.' And he broke down and wept."

Betrayal. Some imagine that betrayal must be an act of national recognition to be real. In fact, betrayal occurs whenever one individual determines to deny truth, liberty, and justice. Betrayal is most offensive when it is perpetrated by those trusted to uphold it the most. Peter betrayed the Christ by denying he knew him yet those who crucified the Christ received a prayer on their behalf from the lips of Christ himself. They acted in ignorance; Peter understood who Jesus was yet acted in his own self interest. Ultimately, that is the root of betrayal; concern with self over any other person or principle of life.

DOCTRINE: CANONS OF DORT (1619)

Head 3, Article 1, Man was originally formed after the image of God. His understanding was adorned with a true and saving knowledge of his Creator and of spiritual things; his heart and will were upright; all his affections pure; and the whole man was holy; but revolting from God by the instigation of the devil, and abusing the freedom of his own will, he forfeited these excellent gifts; and on the contrary entailed on himself blindness of mind, horrible darkness, vanity and perverseness of judgment, became wicked, rebellious, and obdurate in heart and will, and impure in his affections.

[33]

Question: **How can we expect God to bless our preparations for war when so many godless soldiers are in our ranks?**
Answer:
1. *It is certainly a sad state of affairs and should be lamented. It is a situation the Commanders and elected officials must remedy.*
2. *Yet, praise God, we have multitudes of godly and eminent Christians that are among the ranks of our military.*
3. *We also know that God makes use of wicked men to serve according to His providential plan, just as he uses wicked spirits for His purpose.*
4. *We have instances of bad men that have done good service to God and His Church such as the Benjaminites who twice beat the Israelites in Judges 20, The Assyrians that besieged Jerusalem in Isaiah 37:36, Saul, Joab, and even the emperor Constantine, etc.*

THOUGHTS FOR INSPIRATION:·
"The king's heart is a stream of water in the hand of the LORD; he turns it wherever he will." *Proverbs 21:1*

"The summer soldier and the sunshine patriot will, in this crisis, shrink from the service of their country." *Thomas Paine*

"Whatever is, is in its causes just." *John Dryden, Oedipus (act III, sc. 1)*

"Behind the dim unknown,
Standeth God with the shadow, keeping watch above his own." *James Russell Lowell, The Present Crisis (st. 8)*

"I always consider the settlement of America with reverence and wonder, as the opening of a grand scene and design in providence, for the illumination of the ignorant and the emancipation of the slavish part of mankind all over the earth." *John Adams 1735-1826, Second President of the USA*

"It is easier to discover a deficiency in individuals, in states, and in providence, than to see their real import and value." *Georg Hegel 1770-1831, German Philosopher*

"The ultimate triumph of philosophy would be to cast light upon the mysterious ways in which providence moves to achieve the designs it has for man." *Marquis De Sade 1740-1814*

"In the book of life every page has two sides: we human beings fill the upper side with our plans, hopes and wishes, but providence writes on the other side, and what it ordains is seldom our goal." *Nisami*

"Accept the place the divine providence has found for you, the society of your contemporaries, the connection of events." *Ralph Waldo Emerson 1803-1882, American Poet*

REFLECTION: GOOD FAITH

This virtue refers to our relationship to truth. Once the truth of a matter is discovered, a man simply cannot act contrary to truth as if he believes a lie. A man in possession of good faith considers his alternatives before he commits and once he has committed himself his "yes" remains "yes" and his "no" remains "no". Were he to act contrary to an established truth he would be committing an act of virtual "soul suicide". A man of *good faith* will seek to integrate his faith with his life, his character with his activities, and the truth with his own beliefs. He respects the essence of life and seeks to nourish his own spirit by feeding on truth and exercising his virtue.

THOUGHTS FOR STUDY AND MEDITATION: PSALM 94:8-11

"Understand, O dullest of the people! Fools, when will you be wise? He who planted the ear, does he not hear? He who formed the eye, does he not see? He who disciplines the nations, does he not rebuke? He who teaches man knowledge— the LORD—knows the thoughts of man, that they are but a breath."

Psalm 94 assures us that God will punish evil. No act is out of God's view. Some may try to argue that God either has no control over creation or that he is the author of evil. First, Scripture and experience teach us that God preserves His creation by His power (Psalm 104:14; 135:5-7; Acts 14:17, etc). That is, He keeps us alive. Second, Scripture and experience teach us that God has His hand on history and has caused nations to rise and fall according to His will for His purpose and glory. Men may desire to place the guilt of their own moral indiscretion upon God to flee from their own accountability. In fact, God is being patient and allowing for men to take the opportunity to repent and turn from wickedness, the wickedness that springs from a heart in rebellion against God. That rebellion is the evil that plagues the earth. The stubborn and self-indulgent heart of man is the origination of evil, not the good intentions of God, yet, He is able to use the evil of men to accomplish His good purpose as Joseph said, *"What you meant for evil, God has intended for good"* (Genesis 50:20; cf. 45:5-8)

DOCTRINE: WESTMINSTER CONFESSION OF FAITH

V.4, The almighty power, unsearchable wisdom, and infinite goodness of God so far manifest themselves in His providence, that it extendeth itself even to the first fall, and all other sins of angels and men; and that not by a bare permission, but such as hath joined with it a most wise and powerful bounding, and otherwise ordering, and governing of them, in a manifold dispensation, to His own holy ends; yet so, as the sinfulness thereof proceedeth only from the creature, and not from God, who, being most holy and righteous, neither is nor can be the author or approver of sin.

[34]

Question: **Should we expect soldiers to tear down those pagan idols and apostate symbols of false belief that mislead men both in our own nation and beyond our boarders?**
Answer:
1. *Since the sword of religious reform is not in the soldiers' hands, it is not the soldiers' place or responsibility to destroy religious symbols and places of worship in his work as a soldier. God has not removed the authority of the state and soldiers must not usurp the state by tearing down religious institutions no matter their false teaching.*
2. *Treaties and agreements between nations have provided for the safe preservation of religious places and soldiers must act in accordance with our nations treaties while in the service of our government.*

THOUGHTS FOR INSPIRATION:

"The legitimate powers of government extend to such acts only as are injurious to others. But it does me no injury for my neighbor to say there are twenty gods or no god. It neither picks my pocket, nor breaks my leg."

Thomas Jefferson

"We hold it for a fundamental and undeniable truth, that religion, or the duty we owe our Creator and the manner of discharging it, can be directed only by reason and conviction, not by force or violence. The religion then of every man must be left to the conviction and conscience of every man; and it is the right of every man to exercise it as these may dictate. This right is in its nature an unalienable right."
James Madison

"Those people who will not be governed by God will be ruled by tyrants."
William Penn

"Men never do evil so completely and cheerfully as when they do it from religious conviction."
Blaise Pascal
French mathematician and philosopher

REFLECTION: TOLERATION

The virtue of tolerance is not defined by indifference. Tolerance does not tolerate lawlessness or vice. What is tolerable is the conscience of each individual to believe what they freely choose. Tolerance does not establish all supposed truths to be equal. It does not negate the need to exercise judgment in truth discovery and it does not violate the virtues of courage or purity. A man can only be truly tolerant if he also has the virtue of respect and good faith. Tolerance assumes that God will be the final arbiter of justice in the last day and is content to do its duty without engaging in any criminal or un-virtuous behavior before that day arrives.

THOUGHTS FOR STUDY & MEDITATION: DANIEL 3:1,4-6,13-18

"King Nebuchadnezzar made an image of gold, whose height was sixty cubits and its breadth six cubits. He set it up on the plain of Dura, in the province of Babylon. And the herald proclaimed aloud, 'You are commanded, O peoples, nations, and languages, that when you hear the sound of the horn, pipe, lyre, trigon, harp, bagpipe, and every kind of music, you are to fall down and worship the golden image that King Nebuchadnezzar has set up. And whoever does not fall down and worship shall immediately be cast into a burning fiery furnace.' Then Nebuchadnezzar in furious rage commanded that Shadrach, Meshach, and Abednego be brought. So they brought these men before the king. Nebuchadnezzar answered and said to them, "Is it true, O Shadrach, Meshach, and Abednego, that you do not serve my gods or worship the golden image that I have set up? Now if you are ready when you hear the sound of the horn, pipe, lyre, trigon, harp, bagpipe, and every kind of music, to fall down and worship the image that I have made, well and good. But if you do not worship, you shall immediately be cast into a burning fiery furnace. And who is the god who will deliver you out of my hands?"

Daniel and his friends had been taken from the homes of their youth to Babylon. While there, they were exposed to pagan religions and were entered into an indoctrination program. Daniel and his friends resisted the program and while cooperating as far as they could, they stopped short of worshipping false gods. This infuriated their captors and their intolerance for Daniels faith resulted in a short trial and a decision to execute by fire in the furnace. God's saw Daniel's faithfulness and personal piety and used this occasion to demonstrate his providential protection beyond ordinary human means. All of the condemned were saved by God after they were thrown in. The result was more than Daniel could have accomplished no matter how great his argument or how powerful his army. By his own obedience, God used the occasion to change unbelievers minds about the true God. Man can suppress the practice and destroy the architecture and idols of false religion but only God can destroy the lie.

DOCTRINE: CANONS OF DORT

Head 3, Article 16, Concerning Regeneration: But as man by the fall did not cease to be a creature endowed with understanding and will, nor did sin which pervaded the whole race of mankind deprive him of the human nature, but brought upon him depravity and spiritual death; so also this grace of regeneration does not treat men as senseless stocks and blocks, nor takes away their will and its properties, neither does violence thereto; but spiritually quickens, heals, corrects, and at the same time sweetly and powerfully bends it; that where carnal rebellion and resistance formerly prevailed, a ready and sincere spiritual obedience begins to reign, in which the true and spiritual restoration and freedom of our will consist. Wherefore unless the admirable Author of every good work wrought in us, man could have no hope of recovering from his fall by his own free will, by the abuse of which, in a state of innocence, he plunged himself into ruin.

[35]

Question: **What do you say about Valor and Courage?**
Answer:
1.   *I say it is a most noble and heroic virtue, which makes some men differ from others, as much as all men differ from animals.*
2.   *I say, it is impossible for any to be a good soldier without these cardinal virtues: an Army of stags (deer) led by a Lion, is better than an Army of Lions led by a Stag. And, an Army of Children led by a man, is better than an army of men led by a child.*

3. *I say, that one valiant man in an Army is better than a thousand cowards.*

4. *I say, that a coward degenerates from man, being of a base and ignoble nature.*

   a. *God took special care, that all faint-hearted cowards should be discharged for His Armies, Deuteronomy 20:8.*

   b. *Cowards always do more harm than good, being like an X before an L in the Roman numerals (XL).*

   c. *And for the most part, cowards die sooner than the courageous.*

THOUGHTS FOR INSPIRATION:

"Courage is reckoned the greatest of all virtues; because, unless a man has that virtue, he has no security for preserving any other."   *Samuel Johnson*

"Courage is like love: it must have hope for nourishment."
Napoleon Bonaparte

"Untutored courage is useless in the face of educated bullets."
Gen. George S. Patton

"Courage is not the absence of fear, but rather the judgment that something else is more important than fear."   *Ambrose Redmoon*

"Courage is what it takes to stand up and speak; courage is also what it takes to sit down and listen."   *Winston Churchill*

"It is curious that physical courage should be so common in the world and moral courage so rare."   *Mark Twain*

"Courage is doing what you're afraid to do. There can be no courage unless you're scared."   *Edward Vernon Rickenbacker*

"Courage is not simply one of the virtues, but the form of every virtue at the testing point."   *C.S. Lewis*

"One man with courage makes a majority."   *Andrew Jackson*

"Valor is stability, not of legs and arms, but of courage and the soul."
Michel de Montaigne

"When we are afraid we ought not to occupy ourselves with endeavoring to prove that there is no danger, but in strengthening ourselves to go on in spite of the danger."   *Mark Rutherford*

"True courage is not the brutal force of vulgar heroes, but the firm resolve of virtue and reason."   *Alfred North Whitehead*

"It is easy to be brave from a safe distance."   *Aesop*

"Bravery is the capacity to perform properly even when scared half to death."   *Omar N. Bradley*

"Courage is fear holding on a minute longer."   *Gen. George S. Patton*

"I am convinced that a light supper, a good night's sleep, and a fine morning, have sometimes made a hero of the same man, who, by an indigestion, a restless night, and rainy morning, would have proved a coward."
Lord Chesterfield

REFLECTION: COURAGE

"Last, but by no means least, courage-moral courage, is the courage of one's convictions, the courage to see things through. The world is in a constant conspiracy against the brave. It's the age-old struggle-the roar of the crowd on one side and the voice of your conscience on the other."
General Douglas MacArthur

All the other virtues of a soldier need courage if they are to ever find practical expression. Courage sets between the two extremes of cowardice on the one side and foolishness on the other. Not every act of sacrifice ought to be called "courage" and not every act of self-preservation can be called "courage" either. Genuine courage must be informed by the virtues of "fidelity" and "prudence". That is, courage must have a memory and a hope.

If courage has no memory, then it has no reason to hold a conviction or passion to sacrifice for. It becomes an heroic and brave act without substance or attachment to any idea or ideal. If courage has no hope, then it becomes a senseless act of desperation without any expectation that the act will count for anything once it has passed. These ideas about courage generally apply to *"physical courage"* but a soldier must also possess *"moral courage"* and *"intellectual"* courage (i.e., lucidity) as well. Without a commitment to virtue (moral courage) and a commitment to believe nothing but the truth (intellectual courage), physical courage has nothing to stand for. Andre Comte-Sponville suggests that an anatomy of courage might include, "The courage to persist and endure, to live and die, to hold out, fight, resist, persevere."[9] This commentary is only helpful when we can define *"Why"* we persist and endure, *"For What"* we are willing to live and die, and *"When"* we must fight, resist, and persevere.

Courage can only exist in the present. It is action. Cowards *"hope"* to be courageous while the courageous *"are"* in everything they do.

THOUGHTS FOR STUDY & MEDITATION: Deuteronomy 20:1-4,8,9

"When you go out to war against your enemies, and see horses and chariots and an army larger than your own, you shall not be afraid of them, for the LORD your God is with you, who brought you up out of the land of Egypt. And when you draw near to the battle, the priest shall come forward and speak to the people and shall say to them, 'Hear, O Israel, today you are drawing near for battle against your enemies: let not your heart faint. Do not fear or panic or be in dread of them, for the LORD your God is he who goes with you to fight for you against your enemies, to give you the victory... And the officers shall speak further to the people, and say, 'Is there any man who is fearful and fainthearted? Let him go back to his house, lest he make the heart of his fellows melt like his own.' And when the officers have finished speaking to the people, then commanders shall be appointed at the head of the people."

As much as men must prepare for war, only God can bring the victory. History has given us countless stories of inexplicable victories won by men made brave in their faith that God was with them in their cause. No arsenal or weapon of mass destruction can thwart the will of God. No man can be taken from this life before His heavenly Father calls him home. Be it in battle or in bed, a man will die on the day that is appointed. So courage in battle is a simple recognition that God alone is the custodian of our life and if our cause is just and our hearts are pure, then He fights with us. With this in mind, the officers instructed those who could not understand to go home. They were more of a detriment and a distraction than a help.

DOCTRINE: SYNOD OF DORT

ARTICLE 12, This certainty of perseverance, however, is so far from exciting in believers a spirit of pride or of rendering them carnally secure, that on the contrary, it is the real source of humility, filial reverence, true piety, patience in every tribulation, fervent prayers, constancy in suffering, and in confessing the truth, and of solid rejoicing in God; so that the consideration of this benefit should serve as an incentive to the serious and constant practice of gratitude and good works, as appears from the testimonies of Scripture and the examples of the saints.

[36]

Question: **What are the chief reasons to argue for a soldier being courageous in the service of his country?**
Answer:
1. *Because of the worth of the cause which no doubt is God's cause.*
2. *The assurance from the Scriptures that God will not abandon His people when they are striving to do His will.*
3. *The success of our forefathers when they struggled against evil in times past.*
4. *The promise that not one hair can fall from our head without the express knowledge of God.*
5. *The dangers described to the fainthearted or half hearted man, that whoever seeks to preserve his own life in these difficult times actually forfeits it.*
6. *The prayers of God's people are everywhere surrounding this war seeking His blessing and victory.*
7. *The promise of the great reward of honor both in this life and the next, to those who serve not recklessly but selflessly for a cause greater than themselves.*

THOUGHTS FOR INSPIRATION:
"Do your duty and leave the rest to Providence."   *Thomas (Stonewall) Jackson*

"The Lord gets his best soldiers out of the highlands of affliction."
                                                            Charles H. Spurgeon

"Americans, indeed all freemen, remember that in the final choice, a soldier's pack is not so heavy a burden as a prisoner's chains."   *Dwight Eisenhower*

"Faith is to believe what you do not see; the reward of this faith is to see what you believe."   *Saint Augustine*

"He that takes truth for his guide, and duty for his end, may safely trust to God's providence to lead him aright."   *Blaise Pascal*

"Shall ignorance of good and ill Dare to direct the eternal will? Seek virtue, and of that possest, To Providence resign the rest."   *John Gay*

REFLECTION: FAITH

"Faith is not what some people think it is. Their human dream is a delusion. Because they observe that faith is not followed by good works or a better life, they fall into error, even though they speak and hear much about faith. 'Faith is not enough,' they say, 'You must do good works, you must be pious to be saved.' They think that, when you hear the gospel, you start working, creating by your own strength a thankful heart which says, 'I believe.' That is what they think true faith is. But, because this is a human idea, a dream, the heart never learns anything from it, so it does nothing and reform doesn't come from this 'faith,' either."

Instead, faith is God's work in us that changes us and gives new birth from God. (John 1:13). It kills the Old Adam and makes us completely different people. It changes our hearts, our spirits, our thoughts and all our powers. It brings the Holy Spirit with it. Yes, it is a living, creative, active and powerful thing, this faith. Faith cannot help doing good works constantly. It doesn't stop to ask if good works ought to be done, but before anyone asks, it already has done them and continues to do them without ceasing. Anyone who does not do good works in this manner is an unbeliever. He stumbles around and looks for faith and good works, even though he does not know what faith or good works are. Yet he gossips and chatters about faith and good works with many words.

Faith is *a living, bold trust in God's grace, so certain of God's favor that it would risk death a thousand times trusting in it.* Such confidence and knowledge of God's grace makes you happy, joyful and bold in your relationship to God and all creatures. The Holy Spirit makes this happen through faith. Because of it, you freely, willingly and joyfully do good to everyone, serve everyone, suffer all kinds of things, love and praise the God who has shown you such grace. Thus, it is just as impossible to separate faith and works as it is to separate heat and light from fire! Therefore, watch out for your own false ideas and guard against good-for-nothing gossips, who think they're smart enough to define faith and works, but really are the greatest of fools.

Ask God to work faith in you, or you will remain forever without faith, no matter what you wish, say or can do."[10]

STUDY AND MEDITATION: ROMANS 8:28-29

"And we know that for those who love God all things work together for good, for those who are called according to his purpose. [29]For those whom he foreknew he also predestined to be conformed to the image of his Son, in order that he might be the firstborn among many brothers."

"Providence" is a word that describes God's relation to His creation. Many believe that God created the world and then backed away to watch and see what would happen. A more accurate view is that God created and has

stayed involved with His creation. In Romans 8, the providence of God is explained as active rather than passive. God is not working to make the best of a situation, he works everything together for good. There is only one way that God can tie all of the varied activities on the earth together and that is if He is in control of all things. This brings a great comfort to those engaged in dangerous occupations. With an assurance that there is only one day appointed for them to die and that until that day, not one hair can escape from their scalp without God's knowledge of it, those who face danger can summon courage and confidence that remaining in God's will, even death is not intended for their ill but will be a blessing in the day that God intends it.

DOCTRINE: SECOND HELVETIC CONFESSION (1566)

XVI.1, What Is Faith? Christian faith is not an opinion or human conviction, but a most firm trust and a clear and steadfast assent of the mind, and then a most certain apprehension of the truth of God presented in the Scriptures and in the Apostles' Creed, and thus also of God himself, the greatest good, and especially of God's promise and of Christ who is the fulfillment of all promises.

Faith Is the Gift of God. But this faith is a pure gift of God which God alone of his grace gives to his elect according to his measure when, to whom and to the degree he wills. And he does this by the Holy Spirit by means of the preaching of the Gospel and steadfast prayer.

The Increase of Faith. This faith also has its increase, and unless it were given by God, the apostles would not have said: "Lord, increase our faith" (Luke 17:5).

[37]

Question: **What are the principal enemies to courage and valor?**
Answer:
1. *A lack of experience: fresh-water soldiers are commonly fainthearted soldiers, whereas they that have been used to the War, are usually hardened by it.*
2. *Lack of metal: some men's spirits are naturally so low and base, that they will never prove good soldiers: as it is with Gamecocks, so it is among men, there is a breed and generation of warriors.*
3. *Lack of Faith: when a man has only a little or no confidence in God, his heart fails him when he faces danger, whereas Faith has no fear even in the valley of the shadow of death.*

4. *Lack of innocence and a good conscience, Proverbs 28:1. The weight of a man's sin and his lack of reconciliation to God can make him afraid to die in battle for fear of his fate.*

5. *Lack of wisdom and consideration: if men seriously considered the evils of cowardice, and the excellence of valor, it would make them hate the one and strive for the other.*

THOUGHTS FOR INSPIRATION:

"Valor is a gift. Those having it never know for sure whether they have it till the test comes. And those having it in one test never know for sure if they will have it when the next test comes."   *Carl Sandburg*

"Valor is stability, not of legs and arms, but of courage and the soul."

Michel de Montaine

"Perfect Valor is to do, without a witness, all that we could do before the whole world."   *Francois De La Rochefoucculd*

"Valor grows by daring, fear by holding back."   *Publilius Syrus*

"July 3, 1863. ...We built fires all over the battle field and the dead of the blue and gray were being buried all night, and the wounded carried to the hospital. We made no distinction between our own and the confederate wounded, but treated them both alike, and although we had been engaged in fierce and deadly combat all day and weary and all begrimed with smoke and powder and dust, many of us went around among the wounded and gave cooling water or hot coffee to drink. The confederates were surprised and so expressed themselves that they received such kind treatment at our hands, and some of the slightly wounded were glad they were wounded and our prisoners.

But in front of our breastworks, where the confederates were massed in large numbers, the sight was truly awful and appalling. The shells from our batteries had told with fearful and terrible effect upon them and the dead in some places were piled upon each other, and the groans and moans of the wounded were truly saddening to hear. Some were just alive and gasping, but unconscious. Others were mortally wounded and were conscious of the fact that they could not live long; and there were others wounded, how bad they could not tell, whether mortal or otherwise, and so it was they would linger on some longer and some for a shorter time-without the sight or consolation of wife, mother, sister or friend. I saw a letter sticking out of the breast pocket of one of the confederate dead, a young man apparently about *twenty-four. Curiosity prompted me to read it. It was from his young wife away down in the state of Louisiana. She was hoping and longing that this cruel war would end and he could come home, and she says, "Our little boy gets into my lap and says, `Now, Mama, I will give you a kiss for Papa.' But oh how I wish you could come home and kiss me for yourself." But this is only one in a thousand. But such is war and we are getting used to it and can look on scenes of war, carnage and suffering with but very little feeling and without a shudder."*[11] *Corporal Horatio D. Chapman*

"Accepting does not necessarily mean 'liking,' 'enjoying,' or 'condoning.' I can accept what is—and be determined to evolve from there. It is not acceptance but denial that leaves me stuck." *Nathaniel Branden, American psychologist*

REFLECTION: ACCEPTANCE

Acceptance is nothing like surrender. Acceptance is an intellectual virtue that requires the skills of observation and adjustment. Surrender means that you lack an investment in the process and you give the course and setting of your life to someone else. Acceptance is like looking at the road while driving. Staying in the road is not surrender; it is accepting that we must travel on the paths provided. Surrender would be to let go of the steering and allow ourselves to be carried off the side. Only those with confidence and courage can accept the world as it is given to them and find their place in it while retaining a hope for their own happiness.

STUDY AND MEDITATION: JOB 40:1-9

[1]And the LORD said to Job:
[2]"Shall a faultfinder contend with the Almighty?
  He who argues with God, let him answer it."
[3]Then Job answered the LORD and said:
[4]"Behold, I am of small account; what shall I answer you?
  I lay my hand on my mouth.
[5]I have spoken once, and I will not answer;
  twice, but I will proceed no further."
[6]Then the LORD answered Job out of the whirlwind and said:
[7]"Dress for action a like a man;
  I will question you, and you make it known to me.
[8]Will you even put me in the wrong?
  Will you condemn me that you may be in the right?
[9]Have you an arm like God,
  and can you thunder with a voice like his?"

In the book of Job, the main character, Job, is vexed about his misfortunes. He had been a man of wealth and social standing, well known for his virtue and righteous conduct. One tragedy after another left him penniless, friendless, and alone. He began to question God. He couldn't understand God's reason for heaping all of this misfortune on him when he had lived a better life than any of his neighbors. God answered Job with a question. God asked Job why he contended or struggled against Him. Job had entered into a struggle against God. Discontent with God's wisdom in the matters of life, Job had asked questions of God as if he might have been able to improve upon God's work. God took Job to the top of the mountains and gave him a tour. He suggested that Job demonstrate his own creative power and he asked if Job had any part in creating all that he saw. Job had a new perspective. He hadn't become indifferent but he did accept that it was God's will and we might not understand what He does at all times, but we know that His will is best for all times.

DOCTRINE: BELGIC CONFESSION

ARTICLE 13, We believe that this good God, after He had created all things, did not abandon them or give them up to fortune or chance, but that according to His holy will He so rules and governs them that in this world nothing happens without His direction. Yet God is not the Author of the sins which are committed nor can He be charged with them. For His power and goodness are so great and beyond understanding that He ordains and executes His work in the most excellent and just manner, even when devils and wicked men act unjustly. And as to His actions surpassing human understanding, we will not curiously inquire farther than our capacity allows us. But with the greatest humility and reverence we adore the just judgments of God, which are hidden from us, and we content ourselves that we are pupils of Christ, who have only to learn those things which He teaches us in His Word, without transgressing these limits.

This doctrine gives us unspeakable consolation, for we learn thereby that nothing can happen to us by chance, but only by the direction of our gracious heavenly Father. He watches over us with fatherly care, keeping all creatures so under His power that not one hair of our head - for they are all numbered - nor one sparrow can fall to the ground without the will of our Father (*Matthew 10:29-30*). In this we trust, because we know that He holds in check the devil and all our enemies so that they cannot hurt us without His permission and will.

We therefore reject the damnable error of the Epicureans, who say that God does not concern Himself with anything but leaves all things to chance.

[38]

Question: Is there any great need of a soldier possessing a particular skill and cunning in the profession of Arms.
Answer: *Yes: for David thankfully acknowledged the Lords goodness in teaching him how to fight and engage in battle. Psalm 144:1*
1. *Great wisdom, policy, and experience is required in Commanders.*
2. *And no less skill and dexterity in common Soldiers; they must know how to handle their Arms, how to keep Ranks, etc.*
3. *Certainly a few well-trained Soldiers are better than a multitude of raw and inexperienced men.*

THOUGHTS FOR INSPIRATION:

"Quality is never an accident; it is always the result of high intention, sincere effort, intelligent direction and skillful execution; it represents the wise choice of many alternatives." *Willa A. Foster*

"To many a man, and sometimes to a youth, there comes the opportunity to choose between honorable competence and tainted wealth. The young man who starts out to be poor and honorable, holds in his hand one of the strongest elements of success." *Orison Swett Marden*

"Every man passed through my hands and he was told that nothing more remained for him to know, if only he did not forget what he had learned. Thus he was given confidence in himself, the foundations of bravery." *General Alexander Suvarov*

"There is nothing so likely to produce peace as to be well prepared to meet the enemy." *General George Washington*

"I must study politics and war that my sons may have liberty to study mathematics and philosophy. My sons ought to study mathematics and philosophy, geography, natural history, naval architecture, navigation, commerce and agriculture in order to give their children a right to study painting, poetry, music, architecture, statuary, tapestry, and porcelain." *John Adams*

REFLECTION: DISCIPLINE

Discipline is a commitment or a decision to keep certain principles of life and habits of virtue no matter what extenuating circumstances may arise. Discipline is a recognition of an objective. "Discipline" describes a decision to endure hardship, suffering, defamation, personal investment, sacrifice, and to labor towards keeping a principle. A disciplined soldier is one who has a reputation for stability and faithfulness. While others remain unquantifiable, a disciplined soldier can be described in the noblest of terms. A disciplined soldier does what he says. He is described with terms such as steady, stable, reliable, and dependable.

Discipline can only be found in the execution of the habit. It cannot be promised as much as it can be shown. Discipline travels well worn paths of habits.

STUDY AND MEDITATION: JOB 5:17-20

[17] *"Behold, blessed is the one whom God reproves;*
therefore despise not the discipline of the Almighty.
[18] *For he wounds, but he binds up;*
he shatters, but his hands heal.
[19] *He will deliver you from six troubles;*
in seven no evil[a] shall touch you.
[20] *In famine he will redeem you from death,*
and in war from the power of the sword."

"Eliphaz gives to Job a word of caution and exhortation: Despise not thou the chastening of the Almighty. Call it a chastening, which comes from the Father's love, and is for the child's good; and notice it as a messenger from Heaven. Eliphaz also encourages Job to submit to his condition. A good man is happy though he be afflicted, for he has not lost his enjoyment of God, nor his title to heaven; nay, he is happy because he is afflicted. Correction mortifies his corruptions, weans his heart from the world, draws him nearer to God, brings him to his Bible, brings him to his knees. Though God wounds, yet he supports his people under afflictions, and in due time delivers them. Making a wound is sometimes part of a cure. Eliphaz gives Job precious promises of what God would do for him, if he humbled himself. Whatever troubles good men may be in, they shall do them no real harm. Being kept from sin, they are kept from the evil of trouble. And if the servants of Christ are not delivered from outward troubles, they are delivered by them, and while overcome by one trouble, they conquer all. Whatever is maliciously said against them shall not hurt them. They shall have wisdom and grace to manage their concerns. The greatest blessing, both in our employments and in our enjoyments, is to be kept from sin. They

shall finish their course with joy and honor. That man lives long enough
who has done his work, and is fit for another world. It is a mercy to die
seasonably, as the corn is cut and housed when fully ripe; not till then, but
then not suffered to stand any longer. Our times are in God's hands; it is well
they are so. Believers are not to expect great wealth, long life, or to be free
from trials. But all will be ordered for the best. And remark from Job's
history, that steadiness of mind and heart under trial, is one of the highest
attainments of faith. There is little exercise for faith when all things go well.
But if God raises a storm, permits the enemy to send wave after wave, and
seemingly stands aloof from our prayers, then, still to hang on and trust
God, when we cannot trace him, this is the patience of the saints. Blessed
Savior! how sweet it is to look unto thee, the Author and Finisher of faith, in
such moments!"[12]

DOCTRINE: SECOND HELVETIC CONFESSION
XII.1, The Will of God is Explained for us in the Law of God. We teach
that the will of God is explained for us in the law of God, what he wills or
does not will us to do, what is good and just, or what is evil and unjust.
Therefore, we confess that the law is good and holy.

The Law of Nature. And this law was at one time written in the hearts of
men by the finger of God (Rom. 2:15), and is called the law of nature (*the
law of Moses is in two Tables*), and at another it was inscribed by his finger
on the two Tables of Moses, and eloquently expounded in the books of
Moses (Ex. 20:1 ff.; Deut. 5:6 ff.). For the sake of clarity we distinguish the
moral law which is contained in the Decalogue or two Tables and
expounded in the books of Moses, the ceremonial law which determines the
ceremonies and worship of God, and the judicial law which is concerned
with political and domestic matters.

The Law is Complete and Perfect. We believe that the whole will of God
and all necessary precepts for every sphere of life are taught in this law. For
otherwise the Lord would not have forbidden us to add or to take away
anything from this law; neither would he have commanded us to walk in a
straight path before this law, and not to turn aside from it by turning to the
right or to the left (Deut. 4:2; 12:32).

[39]

Question: **What should be done to ensure that soldiers are well trained in their skills?**
Answer:

1. *Officers should be very diligent to teach them and to keep them fit.*
2. *Every soldier should take it upon himself to learn and discover whatever will help them to succeed and survive.*
3. *Every soldier should seek God in prayer, so that God will instruct and teach him: for it is the blessing of God that will make me successful in any profession.*
4. *Whether Commander, Officer, or Enlisted soldier, all may improve themselves by reading and observing what other soldiers have written about war, strategy, survival, and the profession of arms.*

THOUGHTS FOR INSPIRATION:

"Men are wise in proportion, not to their experience, but to their capacity for experience."
James Boswell

"You will find men who want to be carried on the shoulders of others, who think that the world owes them a living. They don't seem to see that we must all lift together and pull together."
Henry Ford

"He who wished to secure the good of others, has already secured his own."
Confucius

"We don't receive wisdom; we must discover it for ourselves after a journey that no one can take for us or spare us."
Marcel Proust

"The leaders who work most effectively, it seems to me, never say 'I.' And that's not because they have trained themselves not to say 'I.' They don't think 'I.' They think 'we'; they think 'team.' They understand their job to be to make the team function. They accept responsibility and don't sidestep it, but 'we' gets the credit.... This is what creates trust, what enables you to get the task done."
Peter Drucker

"An education isn't how much you have committed to memory, or even how much you know. It's being able to differentiate between what you do know and what you don't."
Anatole France

REFLECTION: UNITY

Unity is not a loss of self to the larger whole but a virtue of participation. As the liver, eye, hand, and foot are individual parts of a body so a soldier becomes a part of an integrated whole. Each part of the body retains its uniqueness. A foot never becomes anything else but a foot. The body doesn't devolve into a mass of shapeless flesh. But no single part is able to accomplish a larger goal without a unity of all the parts in a whole. A synthesis of individuality into a larger vision of wholeness creates a unity that multiplies the contribution of each part exponentially. There is no loss of self in unity, only a greater realization of potential.

STUDY AND MEDITATION: LUKE 6:39-41

"³⁹He also told them a parable: "Can a blind man lead a blind man? Will they not both fall into a pit? ⁴⁰A disciple is not above his teacher, but everyone when he is fully trained will be like his teacher. ⁴¹Why do you see the speck that is in your brother's eye, but do not notice the log that is in your own eye?"

There are two important lessons in this passage. The first applies to the teacher. A teacher takes on a tremendous responsibility when he contracts with a student to lead them into knowledge. The student becomes a copy of the teacher and will normally not grow beyond a teacher while under his charge. The competence of a teacher must always be improved upon. Teachers must remain students striving for excellence and perfection in their field. The second applies to the student. Extreme care must be taken by a student lest they develop a false hope in the information imparted to them by a teacher who is not knowledgeable in the area they are teaching.

Finally, for all who look to receive instruction, all men are fallible. There is no other teacher except Jesus Christ who can be completely trusted to give truth to the student. Our goal for the end of life's training is to be like the teacher, Jesus.

DOCTRINE: THE BELGIC CONFESSION

Article 2, By what means God is made known unto us?

We know him by two means: first, by the creation, preservation and government of the universe; which is before our eyes as a most elegant book, wherein all creatures, great and small, are as so many characters leading us to contemplate the invisible things of God, namely, his power and divinity, as the apostle Paul saith, *Romans 1:20*. All which things are sufficient to convince men, and leave them without excuse. Secondly, he makes himself more clearly and fully known to us by his holy and divine Word, that is to say, as far as is necessary for us to know in this life, to his glory and our salvation.

[40]

Question: **How ought Commanders and Officers to conduct themselves towards their Soldiers?**
Answer:
1. *Religiously, showing them no evil example, but being a pattern to them of virtue and godliness, of loyalty and obedience.*
2. *Lovingly, not in a stern and rugged manner, considering that their command is not over Bears, but men.*
3. *Discreetly, encouraging them most that deserve best, and avoiding so much familiarity as may breed contempt.*
4. *Justly, not defrauding them of their due, nor doing or suffering any injury to be done to the worst of them.*

THOUGHTS FOR INSPIRATION:
"Love the soldier and he will love you. That is the secret."
General Alexander Suvarov

"Leadership in the democratic army means firmness, not harshness; understanding, not weakness; justice, not license; humaneness, not intolerance; generosity, not selfishness; pride, not egotism."   *General Omar N. Bradley*

"If you can't get them to salute when they should salute and wear the clothes you tell them to wear, how are you going to get them to die for their country?"
General George S. Patton Jr

"We hail from all corners of the country and have joined together for a common revolutionary objective. And we need the vast majority of the people with us on the road to this objective. . . . Our cadres must show concern for every soldier, and all people in the revolutionary ranks must care for each other, must love and help each other." *Chairman Mao Tsetung*
"Serve the People" (September 8, 1944),
Selected Works, Vol. III, pp. 227-28

"The greatest leader in the world could never win a campaign unless he understood the men he had to lead."   *General Omar Bradley*

"There is an enemy greater than the hospital—the damned fellow who *'doesn't know.'* The hint dropper, riddle poser, the deceiver, the word spinner, the prayer skimper, the two-faced, the mannered, the incoherent. The fellow who *'doesn't know'* has caused a great deal of harm. One is ashamed to talk about him. Arrest for the officer who *'doesn't know'* and house arrest for the field or general officer."   *Gen. Alexander Suvarov*

"I don't mind being called tough, since I find in this racket it's the tough guys who lead the survivors."   *Col. Curtis LeMay*

"Treat people as if they were what they ought to be and you help them to become what they are capable of being."   *Johann Wolfgang Von Goethe*

"Treat a person as he is, and he will remain as he is. Treat him as he could be, and he will become what he should be."   *Jimmy Johnson*

REFLECTION: RESPECT

Respect is more than holding the door open, or saluting an officer of higher rank. It is communication of deeply held convictions. It is a reflection of a person's view of themselves. *"Respect"* is a demanding virtue. It demands not to be taught by preaching but by demonstration. It reproduces itself only when it is used. It is rarely received unless it is first given. It is rarely given unless it is authentic. It seldom can be extended to others when it is not felt by the giver. It is circular among men. It goes round and round and the first to break the circle of mutual respect robs everyone else from its future expression.

Respect is a product of love. It conveys value. It seeks to treat people in such a way that their true nature as children of God, created in His image, is reflected by their treatment of one another.

STUDY AND MEDITATION: MATTHEW 18:1-4

"[1]At that time the disciples came to Jesus, saying, 'Who is the greatest in the kingdom of heaven?' [2]And calling to him a child, he put him in the midst of them [3]and said, 'Truly, I say to you, unless you turn and become like children, you will never enter the kingdom of heaven. [4]Whoever humbles himself like this child is the greatest in the kingdom of heaven.'"

"Christ spoke many words of his sufferings, but only one of his glory; yet the disciples fasten upon that, and overlook the others. Many love to hear and speak of privileges and glory, who are willing to pass by the thoughts of work and trouble. Our Lord set a little child before them, solemnly assuring them, that unless they were converted and made like little children, they could not enter his kingdom. Children, when very young, do not desire authority, do not regard outward distinctions, are free from malice, are teachable, and willingly dependent on their parents. It is true that they soon begin to show other dispositions, and other ideas are taught them at an early age; but these are marks of childhood, and render them proper emblems of the lowly minds of true Christians. Surely we need to be daily renewed in the spirit of our minds, that we may become simple and humble, as little children, and willing to be the least of all. Let us daily study this subject, and examine our own spirits."[13]

DOCTRINE: WESTMINSTER LARGER CATECHISM

129, What is required of superiors towards their inferiors?
It is required of superiors, according to that power they receive from God, and that relation wherein they stand, to love, pray for, and bless their inferiors; to instruct, counsel, and admonish them; countenancing, commending, and rewarding such as do well; and discountenancing, reproving, and chastising such as do ill; protecting, and providing for them all things necessary for soul and body: and by grave, wise, holy, and exemplary carriage, to procure glory to God, honor to themselves, and so to preserve that authority which God hath put upon them.

131, What are the duties of equals?
The duties of equals are, to regard the dignity and worth of each other, in giving honor to go one before another; and to rejoice in each other's gifts and advancement, as their own.

[41]

Question: **How should junior ranking Soldiers present themselves towards their Commanders and Officers?**
Answer:

1. *They must acknowledge and honor them as Superiors, and account them as men set over them by the providence of God, and wisdom of the State.*
2. *They must be exactly obedient to their command, even for conscience sake; Romans 13:5. Of all men, soldiers are most strictly tied to obedience; any lack of obedience may produce very dangerous consequences.*

THOUGHTS FOR INSPIRATION:

"The character of a soldier is high. They who stand forth the foremost in danger, for the community, have the respect of mankind. An officer is much more respected than any other man who has as little money. In a commercial country, money will always purchase respect. But you find, an officer, who has, properly speaking, no money, is every where well received and treated with attention. The character of a soldier always stands him in good stead."

James Boswell

"True humility is intelligent self respect which keeps us from thinking too highly or too meanly of ourselves. It makes us modest by reminding us how far we have come short of what we can be." *Ralph W. Sockman*

"I have no right, by anything I do or say, to demean a human being in his own eyes. What matters is not what I think of him; it is what he thinks of himself. To undermine a man's self-respect is a sin."

Antoine de Saint-Exupery

"If you want to be respected by others the great thing is to respect yourself. Only by that, only by self-respect will you compel others to respect you."

Fyodor Dostoyevsky

REFLECTION: CONTENTMENT

Contentment is defined simply as, *"happiness with your situation in life."* While a true statement, it is not exhaustive. Understanding what contentment *is* may be better illuminated by understanding what contentment *is not*. The opposite of contentment is *envy*. Envy is a desire that is overwhelming to one degree or another. It is a desire that makes the one who envies unhappy and discontent with the present circumstances. Whether it is envy of possessions, position, privilege, or people, i.e., relations, envy distracts a person from the blessings that are already attained. A content person is one who is pleasurable to be around, their motives are pure and selfless, their vision is untainted by ambition and lust and their judgment is clear of confusing goals.

STUDY AND MEDITATION: PSALM 37:16

*"Better is the little that the righteous has
than the abundance of many wicked."*

Contentment is rare in the modern world. The world dependence on consumerism has created a culture of restless malcontents. Where it was once enough to have food on the table, a fire in the hearth, and a roof over our head there is no limit to the list of *necessaries* owed to every free man today.

"In a simpler time, advertising merely called attention to the product and extolled its advantages. Now it manufactures a product of its own: the consumer, perpetually unsatisfied, restless, anxious, and bored. Advertising serves not so much to advertise products as to promote consumption as a way of life. It not only promises to palliate all the old unhappiness to which flesh is heir; it creates or exacerbates new forms of unhappiness-personal insecurity, status anxiety, anxiety in parents about their ability to satisfy the needs of the young. Advertising institutionalizes envy and its attendant anxieties."[14]

DOCTRINE: WESTMINSTER LARGER CATECHISM

Question 147: *What are the duties required in the tenth commandment?*
Answer: The duties required in the tenth commandment are, such a full contentment with our own condition, and such a charitable frame of the whole soul toward our neighbor, as that all our inward motions and affections touching him, tend unto, and further all that good which is his.
Question 148: *What are the sins forbidden in the tenth commandment?*
Answer: The sins forbidden in the tenth commandment are, discontentment with our own estate; envying and grieving at the good of our neighbor, together with all inordinate motions and affections to anything that is his.

[42]

Question: **What do you think of soldiers that are disposed to insubordination?**
Answer:
1. *They are as dangerous a breed that can ever be found in the ranks of an Army.*
2. *They deserve the most sever punishment, and ought to be completely separated from the Army.*
3. *They will hardly ever prove to be good Soldiers when they are possessed with this malcontent and rebellious disposition.*

THOUGHTS FOR INSPIRATION:

"It is easier to fight for principles than to live up to them."   *Alfred Adler,*
Problems of Neurosis

"The depth and strength of a human character are defined by its moral reserves. People reveal themselves completely only when they are thrown out of the customary conditions of their life, for only then do they have to fall back on their reserves."   *Leon Trotsky*

"One of Satan's greatest tools is pride: to cause a man or a woman to center so much attention on self that he or she becomes insensitive to his Creator or fellow beings. It is a cause for discontent, divorce, teenage rebellion, family indebtedness, and most other problems we face."   *Ezra Taft Benson*

"The moment we set our will on rebellion, we lose the right to have control over our mind."   *Joe Campbell*

"In taking revenge, a man is but even with his enemy; but in passing it over he is superior."   *Francis Bacon*

"Latent in every man is a venom of amazing bitterness, a black resentment; something that curses and loathes life, a feeling of being trapped, of having trusted and been fooled, of being the helpless prey of impotent rage, blind surrender, the victim of a savage, ruthless power that gives and takes away, enlists a man, drops him, promises and betrays, and—crowning injury—inflicts on him the humiliation of feeling sorry for himself."   *Paul Valery*

"It has become dramatically clear that the foundation of corporate integrity is personal integrity."   *Sam DiPiazza*
CEO of Pricewaterhouse Coopers

REFLECTION: RELIABILITY

"Reliability" describes the character of one who can be relied on. It describes someone who is faithful and can be trusted. The virtue of "reliability" is very close to the virtue of "fidelity". Perhaps a distinction is that fidelity has to do with remembering whereas reliability has to do with activity. A reliable soldier is one that stays with the work until it is finished or until he is providentially hindered from completing it.

STUDY AND MEDITATION: JEREMIAH 2:18-20

"18And now what do you gain by going to Egypt
  to drink the waters of the Nile?
Or what do you gain by going to Assyria
  to drink the waters of the Euphrates?
19Your evil will chastise you,
  and your apostasy will reprove you.
Know and see that it is evil and bitter
  for you to forsake the LORD your God;
  the fear of me is not in you,
    declares the Lord GOD of hosts.

[20]*"For long ago I broke your yoke*
   and burst your bonds;
   but you said, 'I will not serve.'
yes, on every high hill
   and under every green tree
   you bowed down like a whore."

The people of God were seeking to be refreshed and sustained by drinking the "waters" of other nations when God alone is the only source of refreshment and sustenance. Their memories failed to recall that God had delivered them from the very nations they now turn to for help. In their identification with those nations, they had lost their unique relationship with God. The people were bowing down to the idols of those lands and so were rejecting the yoke of God and taking on the yoke of idols.

DOCTRINE: WESTMINSTER CONFESSION OF FAITH

XX.3, They who, upon pretense of Christian liberty, do practice any sin, or cherish any lust, do thereby destroy the end of Christian liberty; which is, that, being delivered out of the hands of our enemies, we might serve the Lord without fear, in holiness and righteousness before him, all the days of our life.

[43]

Question: **What is your opinion of those Soldiers that are unpatriotic or desert the nation they have promised to serve?**
Answer:
1. *Such are, by the law of our land, deserving of death.*
2. *It is a most ignoble and base behavior to do such a thing, and they who do it deserve to be branded with infamy forever.*
3. *It is foul and wicked, it is offensive both to God and to man, Psalm 78:9.*
   a. *For, such (if the cause is just) abandon the Cause of God.*
   b. *They forsake the public trust which was reposed in them by their nation.*
   c. *They betray the Cause they have vowed to support.*
   d. *They make a dangerous example, and may be the cause of the overthrow of their Commands.*

THOUGHTS FOR INSPIRATION:

"Though those that are betrayed Do feel the treason sharply, yet the traitor Stands in worse case of woe."   *William Shakespeare*

"God defend me from my friends; from my enemies I can defend myself."
                                                              Proverb

"No wise man ever thought that a traitor should be trusted."
                                        Cicero (Marcus Tullius Cicero),
                                        Orationes In Verrem (II, 1, 15)

"Any appeasement of tyranny is treason to this republic and to the democratic ideal."   *William Allen White*

"Is there not some chosen curse, some hidden thunder in the stores of heaven, red with uncommon wrath, to blast the man who owes his greatness to his country's ruin!"   *Joseph Addison*

"A nation can survive its fools, and even the ambitious. But it cannot survive treason from within. An enemy at the gates is less formidable, for he is known and carries his banner openly. But the traitor moves amongst those within the gate freely, his sly whispers rustling through all the alleys, heard in the very halls of government itself. For the traitor appears not a traitor; he speaks in accents familiar to his victims, and he wears their face and their arguments, he appeals to the baseness that lies deep in the hearts of all men. He rots the soul of a nation, he works secretly and unknown in the night to undermine the pillars of the city, he infects the body politic so that it can no longer resist. A murder is less to fear."   *Marcus Tullius Cicero*

REFLECTION: FIDELITY

Fidelity means faithfulness, and is often associated with loyalty, commitment, steadfastness, or allegiance. It is relied on by those around us as a key to understanding our role in a group or society. The future is predictable only as far as we are faithful.

A bridge makes a good metaphor for fidelity in that each of the parts must remain committed to the work of the bridge or the entire structure will fall. If any part of the bridge, that is one of the support or suspensions were to forget their task, the entire bridge would be in danger of collapse.

It is the same with people. When stress comes and presses down on a society such as in times of war, there is no place for any essential part to shrink back from their duty. Without the virtue of fidelity, predicting the response of people to a situation is impossible.

STUDY AND MEDITATION: MATTHEW 26:47-56

"47 While he was still speaking, Judas came, one of the twelve, and with him a great crowd with swords and clubs, from the chief priests and the elders of the people. 48 Now the betrayer had given them a sign, saying, "The one I will kiss is the man; seize him." 49 And he came up to Jesus at once and said, "Greetings, Rabbi!" And he kissed him. 50 Jesus said to him, "Friend, do what you came to do." Then they came up and laid hands on Jesus and seized him. 51 And behold, one of those who were with Jesus stretched out his hand and drew his sword and struck the servant of the high priest and cut off his ear. 52 Then Jesus said to him, "Put your sword back into its place. For all who take the sword will perish by the sword. 53 Do you think that I cannot appeal to my Father, and he will at once send me more than twelve legions of angels? 54 But how then should the Scriptures be fulfilled, that it must be so?" 55 At that hour Jesus said to the crowds, "Have you come out as against a robber, with swords and clubs to capture me? Day after day I sat in the temple teaching, and you did not seize me. 56 But all this has taken place that the Scriptures of the prophets might be fulfilled." Then all the disciples left him and fled."

John Calvin comments, "I have no doubt that Judas was restrained, either by reverence for our Lord, or by shame for his crime, from venturing openly to avow himself as one of the enemies... I conjecture, for this reason, that he recollected the numerous-proofs by which Christ had formerly attested his divine power. But it was, at the same time, astonishing madness, either to attempt to conceal himself by frivolous hypocrisy, when he came into the presence of the Son of God. Luke expresses it more fully: *Judas, betrayest thou the Son of man with a kiss?* except that there is greater force in this reproof, that the benevolence of his Master, and the very high honor conferred on him, are wickedly abused for the purpose of the basest treachery. For Christ does not employ an ironical address when he calls him friend, but charges him with ingratitude, that, from being an intimate friend, who sat at his table, he had become a traitor, as had been predicted in the Psalm: If a stranger had done this, I could have endured it; but now my private and familiar friend, with whom I took food pleasantly, who accompanied me to the temple of the Lord, hath prepared snares against me. This shows clearly—what I hinted a little ago—that, whatever may be the artifices by which hypocrites conceal themselves, and whatever may be the pretenses which they hold out, when they come into the presence of the Lord, their crimes become manifest; and it even becomes the ground of a severer sentence against them, that, having been admitted into the bosom of

Christ, they treacherously rise up against him. For the word friend, as we have stated, contains within itself a sharp sting."

DOCTRINE: HEIDELBERG CATECHISM

Q. 127 *Which is the sixth petition?* (of the Lord's Prayer)
"And lead us not into temptation, but deliver us from evil"; that is, since we are so weak in ourselves, that we cannot stand a moment; and besides this, since our mortal enemies, the devil, the world, and our own flesh, cease not to assault us, do thou therefore preserve and strengthen us by the power of thy Holy Spirit, that we may not be overcome in this spiritual warfare, but constantly and strenuously may resist our foes, till at last we obtain a complete victory.

[44]

Question: **How ought Soldiers to be encouraged and rewarded?**
Answer:
1. *They ought to be highly honored, especially those who have demonstrated courage and fidelity in the service of their Country.*
2. *They ought to be well taken care of, with sufficient pay, while they are deployed: for no man goes to war at his own personal expense for that would be to engage in mercenary war.*
3. *Any who have been injured should be liberally provided for and the families of those who were lost should be comfortably maintained all their days by those who sent them.*

THOUGHTS FOR INSPIRATION:

"I was very careful to send Mr. Roosevelt every few days a statement of our casualties. I tried to keep before him all the time the casualty results because you get hardened to these things and you have to be very careful to keep them always in the forefront of your mind."   *General George C. Marshall*

"The education of a man is never completed until he dies."   *Robert E. Lee*

"What a cruel thing is war: to separate and destroy families and friends, and mar the purest joys and happiness God has granted us in this world; to fill our hearts with hatred instead of love for our neighbors, and to devastate the fair face of this beautiful world."   *Robert E. Lee*

"And like the old soldier in that ballad, I now close my military career and just fade away, an old soldier who tried to do his duty as God gave him the sight to see that duty." *General Douglas MacArthur*

"Part of the American dream is to live long and die young. Only those Americans who are willing to die for their country are fit to live." *Gen. Douglas MacArthur*

"It is foolish and wrong to mourn the men who died. Rather we should thank God that such men lived." *General George S. Patton*

REFLECTION: HONOR

Honor may be defined simply as "having a good name." It is the motivation that drives what men must do. An honorable action is one that has met the criteria of being worthy and worthwhile and an honorable man is one with both the courage to undertake the work and the constancy or fidelity to see it through to completion.

Honor includes other virtues such as courage, integrity, fidelity, respect, selflessness, and duty. It is a general term to describe a specific character. There is no honor without the other virtues. Even if one is "honored" because of their rank or position, they are not necessarily "honorable" in their character. Honor is an assessment made by a community regarding a man's complete character and creed.

STUDY AND MEDITATION: 1 THESSALONIANS 4:3-5

[3]*For this is the will of God, your sanctification: that you abstain from sexual immorality; [4]that each one of you know how to control his own body in holiness and honor, [5]not in the passion of lust like the Gentiles who do not know God"*

Matthew Henry commented that 1 Thessalonians 4 is…, "A caution against uncleanness, this being a sin directly contrary to sanctification, or that holy walking to which he so earnestly exhorts them. This caution is expressed, and also enforced by many arguments,

It is expressed in these words: *That you should abstain from fornication* [i.e., sexual immorality] (v. 3), by which we are to understand all uncleanness whatsoever, either in a married or unmarried state. Adultery is of course included, though fornication is particularly mentioned. And other sorts of uncleanness are also forbidden, of which it is a shame even to speak, though they are done by too many in secret. All that is contrary to chastity in heart, speech, and behavior, is contrary to the command of God in the Decalogue, and contrary to that holiness which the gospel requires.

1. It is the will of God in general that we should be holy, because *he that called us is holy,* and because we are *chosen unto salvation through the sanctification of the Spirit;* and not only does God require holiness in the heart, but also purity in our bodies, and that we should cleanse ourselves from all *filthiness both of flesh and spirit*
2. This will be greatly for our honor: so much is plainly implied, v. 4. Whereas the contrary will be a great dishonor.
3. To indulge the lust of concupiscence is to live and act like heathens.
4. The sin of uncleanness, especially adultery, is a great piece of injustice that God will be the avenger of.
5. The sin of uncleanness is contrary to the nature and design of our Christian calling: *For God hath called us not unto uncleanness, but unto holiness,* v. 7."

DOCTRINE: HEIDELBERG CATECHISM
Q. 108, 109, What doeth the seventh commandment teach us?
That all uncleanness is accursed of God; and that therefore we must with all our hearts detest the same, and live chastely and temperately, whether in holy wedlock or in single life.
Doth God forbid in this commandment only adultery and such like grow sins?
Since both our body and soul are temples of the Holy Ghost, he commands us to preserve them pure and holy; therefore He forbids all unchaste actions.

APPENDIX A

THE SOLDIER'S POCKET BIBLE[15]

Containing the most (if not all) those places in the Scriptures which show the qualifications of the inner man, that is a fit Soldier to fight the Lord's Battles, both before the fight, in the fight, and after the fight;

Those Scriptures are arranged under several heads, and fitly applied to the various circumstances Soldiers will find themselves in.

These may also be useful for all Christians to meditate on in difficult times of war.

"This Book of the Law shall not depart from your mouth, but you shall meditate on it day and night, so that you may be careful to do according to all that is written in it. For then you will make your way prosperous, and then you will have good success." Joshua 1:8

✦ **A Soldier must never behave wickedly.**

> *"When you are encamped against your enemies, then you shall keep yourself from every evil thing."* Deuteronomy 23:9

> *"Soldiers also asked him, "And we, what shall we do?" And he said to them, "Do not extort money from anyone by threats or by false accusation, and be content with your wages."* Luke 3:14

> *"But if in spite of this you will not listen to me, but walk contrary to me, then I will walk contrary to you in fury, and I myself will discipline you sevenfold for your sins."* Leviticus 26:27, 28

> *"They shall stumble over one another, as if to escape a sword, though none pursues. And you shall have no power to stand before your enemies."* Leviticus 26:37

> *"The LORD will cause you to be defeated before your enemies. You shall go out one way against them and flee seven ways before them. And you shall be a horror to all the kingdoms of the earth."* Deuteronomy 28:25

✦ **A Soldier must be valiant for God's cause.**

> *"Then Saul said to David, "Here is my elder daughter Merab. I will give her to you for a wife. Only be valiant for me and fight the LORD's battles.' For Saul thought, 'Let not my hand be against him, but let the hand of the Philistines be against him."*   1 Samuel 18:17

> *"Be of good courage, and let us be courageous for our people, and for the cities of our God, and may the LORD do what seems good to him."*   2 Samuel 10:12

> *""····and that all this assembly may know that the LORD saves not with sword and spear. For the battle is the LORD's, and he will give you into our hand."*   1 Samuel 17:47

✦ **A Soldier must deny his own wisdom, his own strength, and all provision for war.**

> *"Trust in the LORD with all your heart,*
> *   and do not lean on your own understanding."*   Proverbs 3:5

> *"He will guard the feet of his faithful ones,*
> *   but the wicked shall be cut off in darkness,*
> *   for not by might shall a man prevail."*   1 Samuel 2:9

> *"For not in my bow do I trust,*
> *   nor can my sword save me."*   Psalm 44:6

> *"The king is not saved by his great army;*
> *   a warrior is not delivered by his great strength."*   Psalm 33:16

> *"The war horse is a false hope for salvation,*
> *   and by its great might it cannot rescue."*   Psalm 33:17

> *"No man has power to retain the spirit, or power over the day of death. There is no discharge from war, nor will wickedness deliver those who are given to it."*   Ecclesiastes 8:8

> *"O our God, will you not execute judgment on them? For we are powerless against this great horde that is coming against us. We do not know what to do, but our eyes are on you."*   2 Chronicles 20:12

✦ **A Soldier must put his confidence in God's wisdom and strength.**

> *"Finally, be strong in the Lord and in the strength of his might."*
> Ephesians 6:10

> *"With God are wisdom and might;*
> *he has counsel and understanding."*   Job 12:13

> *"Awesome is God from his sanctuary;*
> *the God of Israel—he is the one who gives power and strength to*
> *his people. Blessed be God!"*   Psalm 68:35

> *"God is our refuge and strength,*
> *a very present help in trouble."*   Psalm 46:1

> *"But go, act, be strong for the battle. Why should you suppose that*
> *God will cast you down before the enemy? For God has power to*
> *help or to cast down."*   2 Chronicles 25:8

> *"With the mighty deeds of the Lord GOD I will come;*
> *I will remind them of your righteousness, yours alone."* Psalm 71:16

> *"Then David said to the Philistine, 'You come to me with a sword and*
> *with a spear and with a javelin, but I come to you in the name of the*
> *LORD of hosts, the God of the armies of Israel, whom you have*
> *defied.'"*   1 Samuel 17:45

✦ **A Soldier must pray before he goes to the fight.**

> *"And we prayed to our God and set a guard as a protection against*
> *them day and night."*   Nehemiah 4:9

> *"Then Samson called to the LORD and said, "O Lord GOD, please*
> *remember me and please strengthen me only this once, O God, that*
> *I may be avenged on the Philistines for my two eyes."* Judges 16:28

> *"And it was told David, 'Ahithophel is among the conspirators with*
> *Absalom." And David said, "O LORD, please turn the counsel of*
> *Ahithophel into foolishness.'"*   2 Samuel 15:31

> *"If any of you lacks wisdom, let him ask God, who gives generously*
> *to all without reproach, and it will be given him."*   James 1:5

*"Give me understanding, that I may keep your law
and observe it with my whole heart."*   Psalm 119:34

*"Turn to me and be gracious to me;
give your strength to your servant,
and save the son of your maidservant."*   Psalm 86:16

*"Contend, O LORD, with those who contend with me;
fight against those who fight against me!
Draw the spear and javelin against my pursuers!
Say to my soul, 'I am your salvation!' "*   Psalm 35:1, 3

*"And the people of Israel said to the LORD, "We have sinned; do to
us whatever seems good to you. Only please deliver us this day."*
Judges 10:15

✦ **A Soldier must consider and believe God's gracious promises.**

*"And they rose early in the morning and went out into the
wilderness of Tekoa. And when they went out, Jehoshaphat stood
and said, 'Hear me, Judah and inhabitants of Jerusalem! Believe in
the LORD your God, and you will be established; believe his
prophets, and you will succeed.' "*   2 Chronicles 20:20

*"···for the LORD your God is he who goes with you to fight for you
against your enemies, to give you the victory."*   Deuteronomy 20:4

"The LORD will fight for you, and you have only to be silent."
Exodus 14:14

*"···but you shall fear the LORD your God, and he will deliver you
out of the hand of all your enemies."*   2 Kings 17:39

*"If this be so, our God whom we serve is able to deliver us from the
burning fiery furnace, and he will deliver us out of your hand, O king.
But if not, be it known to you, O king, that we will not serve your gods
or worship the golden image that you have set up."*   Daniel 3:17, 18

*"···from the time that I appointed judges over my people Israel. And
I will subdue all your enemies. Moreover, I declare to you that the
LORD will build you a house."*   1 Chronicles 17:10

*"You shall seek those who contend with you,
but you shall not find them;*

those who war against you
  shall be as nothing at all."   Isaiah 41:12

"...no weapon that is fashioned against you shall succeed,
  and you shall confute every tongue that rises against you in judgment.
This is the heritage of the servants of the LORD
  and their vindication from me, declares the LORD."   Isaiah 54:17

✦ A Soldier must not fear his enemies.

"When you go out to war against your enemies, and see horses and
chariots and an army larger than your own, you shall not be afraid
of them, for the LORD your God is with you, who brought you up
out of the land of Egypt."   Deuteronomy 20:1

"But the LORD said to me, 'Do not fear him, for I have given him
and all his people and his land into your hand. And you shall do to
him as you did to Sihon the king of the Amorites, who lived at
Heshbon.'"   Deuteronomy 3:2

"You shall not fear them, for it is the LORD your God who fights for
you."   Deuteronomy 3:22

"Be strong and courageous. Do not be afraid or dismayed before
the king of Assyria and all the horde that is with him, for there are
more with us than with him. With him is an arm of flesh, but with us
is the LORD our God, to help us and to fight our battles.' And the
people took confidence from the words of Hezekiah king of Judah."
                                                  2 Chronicles 32:7,8

"And say to him, 'Be careful, be quiet, do not fear, and do not let
your heart be faint because of these two smoldering stumps of
firebrands, at the fierce anger of Rezin and Syria and the son of
Remaliah."   Isaiah 7:4

"And do not fear those who kill the body but cannot kill the soul.
Rather fear him who can destroy both soul and body in hell."
                                                  Matthew 10:28

"But I say to you, Love your enemies and pray for those who
persecute you..."   Matthew 5:44

"But Jehu the son of Hanani the seer went out to meet him and said
to King Jehoshaphat, "Should you help the wicked and love those

who hate the LORD? Because of this, wrath has gone out against
you from the LORD."   2 Chronicles 19:2

"Do I not hate those who hate you, O LORD?
  And do I not loathe those who rise up against you?
I hate them with complete hatred;
  I count them my enemies."   Psalm 139:21-22

✦ A Soldier must cry unto God in his heart in the
very instant of the battle.
  "And when Judah looked, behold, the battle was in front of and
  behind them. And they cried to the LORD, and the priests blew the
  trumpets."   2 Chronicles 13:14

  "And Asa cried to the LORD his God, "O LORD, there is none like
  you to help, between the mighty and the weak. Help us, O LORD
  our God, for we rely on you, and in your name we have come
  against this multitude. O LORD, you are our God; let not man
  prevail against you."   2 Chronicles 14:11

  "As soon as the captains of the chariots saw Jehoshaphat, they said,
  'It is the king of Israel' So they turned to fight against him. And
  Jehoshaphat cried out, and the LORD helped him; God drew them
  away from him."   2 Chronicles 18:31

✦ A Soldier must consider that sometimes God's people
have the worst in battle as well as God's enemies.
  "David said to the messenger, 'Thus shall you say to Joab, "Do not
  let this matter trouble you, for the sword devours now one and now
  another. Strengthen your attack against the city and overthrow it."
  And encourage him.'"   2 Samuel 11:25

  "It is the same for all, since the same event happens to the righteous
  and the wicked, to the good and the evil, to the clean and the unclean,
  to him who sacrifices and him who does not sacrifice. As is the good,
  so is the sinner, and he who swears is as he who shuns an oath."
                                                        Ecclesiastes 9:2

  "So about 3,000 men went up there from the people. And they fled
  before the men of Ai..."   Joshua 7:4

"So the Philistines fought, and Israel was defeated, and they fled, every man to his home. And there was a very great slaughter, for there fell of Israel thirty thousand foot soldiers."   1 Samuel 4:10

"Whenever Moses held up his hand, Israel prevailed, and whenever he lowered his hand, Amalek prevailed."   Exodus 17:11

"For these things I weep; my eyes flow with tears;
for a comforter is far from me, one to revive my spirit;
my children are desolate, for the enemy has prevailed."
                                                  Lamentations 1:16

✦ Soldiers and all of us must consider that though God's people have the worst of it, it still comes from the Lord.

"Who gave up Jacob to the looter,
  and Israel to the plunderers?
Was it not the LORD, against whom we have sinned,
  in whose ways they would not walk,
  and whose law they would not obey?"*   Isaiah 42:24

"Is a trumpet blown in a city,
  and the people are not afraid?
Does disaster come to a city,
  unless the LORD has done it?"   Amos 3:6

"And the LORD sold them into the hand of Jabin king of Canaan,
who reigned in Hazor..."   Judges 4:2

"My transgressions were bound into a yoke;
  by his hand they were fastened together;
they were set upon my neck;
  he caused my strength to fail;
the Lord gave me into the hands
  of those whom I cannot withstand."   Lamentations 1:14

"The Lord has scorned his altar,
  disowned his sanctuary;
he has delivered into the hand of the enemy
  the walls of her palaces;
they raised a clamor in the house of the LORD
  as on the day of festival."   Lamentations 2:7

✛ **For their iniquities, God's people are delivered into the hands of their enemies.**

> *"All the nations will say, 'Why has the LORD done thus to this land? What caused the heat of this great anger? Then people will say, 'It is because they abandoned the covenant of the LORD, the God of their fathers, which he made with them when he brought them out of the land of Egypt..."* Deuteronomy 29:24, 25

> *"The LORD said to Joshua, 'Get up! Why have you fallen on your face? Israel has sinned; they have transgressed my covenant that I commanded them; they have taken some of the devoted things; they have stolen and lied and put them among their own belongings.'"* Joshua 7:10, 11

> *"The captain of the guard took Jeremiah and said to him, 'The LORD your God pronounced this disaster against this place. The LORD has brought it about, and has done as he said. Because you sinned against the LORD and did not obey his voice, this thing has come upon you.'"* Jeremiah 40:2, 3

> *"My people have been lost sheep. Their shepherds have led them astray, turning them away on the mountains. From mountain to hill they have gone. They have forgotten their fold. All who found them have devoured them, and their enemies have said, 'We are not guilty, for they have sinned against the LORD, their habitation of righteousness, the LORD, the hope of their fathers.'"* Jeremiah 50:6, 7

> *"Why should a living man complain,*
> *a man, about the punishment of his sins?"* Lamentations 3:39

✛ **Therefore both Soldiers and all God's people upon such occasions must search out their sins.**

> *"Let us test and examine our ways,*
> *and return to the LORD!"* Lamentations 3:40

> *"Get up! Consecrate the people and say, 'Consecrate yourselves for tomorrow; for thus says the LORD, God of Israel, "There are devoted things in your midst, O Israel. You cannot stand before your enemies until you take away the devoted things from among you."* Joshua 7:13

✦ Especially let Soldiers and all of us upon such occasions search whether we have not put two little confidence in the Army of the Lord, and too much in the army of flesh.

> "...or my people have committed two evils:
> they have forsaken me, the fountain of living waters,
> and hewed out cisterns for themselves,
> > broken cisterns that can hold no water." Jeremiah 2:13

> "From it too you will come away
> > with your hands on your head,
> for the LORD has rejected those in whom you trust,
> > and you will not prosper by them." Jeremiah 2:37

> "Thus says the LORD:
> 'Cursed is the man who trusts in man
> > and makes flesh his strength,
> > whose heart turns away from the LORD.'" Jeremiah 17:5

✦ And let Soldiers and all of us consider, that to prevent this sin, and for the committing of this sin, the Scriptures show us that the Lord has ever given the victory to a few.

> "The LORD said to Gideon, 'The people with you are too many for me to give the Midianites into their hand, lest Israel boast over me, saying, "My own hand has saved me."'" Judges 7:2

> "And the LORD said to Gideon, 'With the 300 men who lapped I will save you and give the Midianites into your hand, and let all the others go every man to his home.'" Judges 7:7

> "And the people of Benjamin mustered out of their cities on that day 26,000 men who drew the sword, besides the inhabitants of Gibeah, who mustered 700 chosen men." Judges 20:15

> "And the men of Israel, apart from Benjamin, mustered 400,000 men who drew the sword; all these were men of war." Judges 20:17

> "The people of Benjamin came out of Gibeah and destroyed on that day 22,000 men of the Israelites." Judges 20:21

"And Benjamin went against them out of Gibeah the second day, and destroyed 18,000 men of the people of Israel. All these were men who drew the sword."   Judges 20:25

"And the people of Israel went up against the people of Benjamin on the third day and set themselves in array against Gibeah, as at other times."   Judges 20:30

"Surrounding the Benjaminites, they pursued them and trod them down from Nohah as far as opposite Gibeah on the east" Judges 20:43

"And they turned and fled toward the wilderness to the rock of Rimmon. Five thousand men of them were cut down in the highways. And they were pursued hard to Gidom, and 2,000 men of them were struck down."   Judges 20:45

"So all who fell that day of Benjamin were 25,000 men who drew the sword, all of them men of valor."   Judges 20:46

"Abijah went out to battle, having an army of valiant men of war, 400,000 chosen men. And Jeroboam drew up his line of battle against him with 800,000 chosen mighty warriors. Then Abijah stood up on Mount Zemaraim that is in the hill country of Ephraim and said, "Hear me, O Jeroboam and all Israel!"   2 Chronicles 13:3, 4

"And now you think to withstand the kingdom of the LORD in the hand of the sons of David, because you are a great multitude and have with you the golden calves that Jeroboam made you for gods."   2 Chronicles 13:8

"But as for us, the LORD is our God, and we have not forsaken him. We have priests ministering to the LORD who are sons of Aaron, and Levites for their service."   2 Chronicles 13:10

"Behold, God is with us at our head, and his priests with their battle trumpets to sound the call to battle against you. O sons of Israel, do not fight against the LORD, the God of your fathers, for you cannot succeed."
"Jeroboam had sent an ambush around to come upon them from behind. Thus his troops[a] were in front of Judah, and the ambush was behind them. [14]And when Judah looked, behold, the battle was in front of and behind them. And they cried to the LORD, and the priests blew the trumpets. Then the men of Judah raised the battle shout. And when the men of Judah shouted, God defeated Jeroboam and all Israel before Abijah and Judah."   2 Chronicles 13:12-15

"Abijah and his people struck them with great force, so there fell slain of Israel 500,000 chosen men." 2 Chronicles 3:17

"And Asa had an army of 300,000 from Judah, armed with large shields and spears, and 280,000 men from Benjamin that carried shields and drew bows. All these were mighty men of valor.
Zerah the Ethiopian came out against them with an army of a million men and 300 chariots, and came as far as Mareshah. And Asa went out to meet him, and they drew up their lines of battle in the Valley of Zephathah at Mareshah. And Asa cried to the LORD his God, "O LORD, there is none like you to help, between the mighty and the weak. Help us, O LORD our God, for we rely on you, and in your name we have come against this multitude. O LORD, you are our God; let not man prevail against you." 2 Chronicles 14:8-11

✝And let soldiers, and all of us know, that in the moment that God has promised us help, is precisely when we will see no help come from man.

"So Abraham called the name of that place, "The LORD will provide"; as it is said to this day, "On the mount of the LORD it shall be provided." Genesis 22:14

"And Moses said to the people, "Fear not, stand firm, and see the salvation of the LORD, which he will work for you today. For the Egyptians whom you see today, you shall never see again." Exodus 14:13

"O our God, will you not execute judgment on them? For we are powerless against this great horde that is coming against us. We do not know what to do, but our eyes are on you." 2 Chronicles 20:12

"You will not need to fight in this battle. Stand firm, hold your position, and see the salvation of the LORD on your behalf, O Judah and Jerusalem.' Do not be afraid and do not be dismayed. Tomorrow go out against them, and the LORD will be with you." 2 Chronicles 20:17

"Vengeance is mine, and recompense, for the time when their foot shall slip; for the day of their calamity is at hand, and their doom comes swiftly.'
For the LORD will vindicate his people

and have compassion on his servants,
when he sees that their power is gone
   and there is none remaining, bond or free."
Deuteronomy 32:35, 36

"But he said to me, "My grace is sufficient for you, for my power is
made perfect in weakness." Therefore I will boast all the more
gladly of my weaknesses, so that the power of Christ may rest upon
me."
2 Corinthians 12:9

"Then he said to me, "This is the word of the LORD to Zerubbabel:
Not by might, nor by power, but by my Spirit, says the LORD of
hosts."
Zechariah 4:6

"Because the poor are plundered, because the needy groan, I will now
arise," says the LORD;
   "I will place him in the safety for which he longs."   Psalm 12:5

"Now I will arise," says the LORD,
   "now I will lift myself up;
   now I will be exalted."*
Isaiah 33:10

✦ If our forces were to ever be weakened and our enemies
were to simultaneously grow stronger, then let Soldiers
and all of us know that we had a promise from God that
He would help when we were stronger, and therefore let
us pray more confidently and expect that help to come
when we are weaker.

   "O LORD, be gracious to us; we wait for you.
   Be our arm every morning,
   our salvation in the time of trouble."   Isaiah 33:2

   "Hear, O LORD, the voice of Judah,
   and bring him in to his people.
   With your hands contend for him,
   and be a help against his adversaries."   Deuteronomy 33:7

   "Look to the right and see:
   there is none who takes notice of me;
   no refuge remains to me;
   no one cares for my soul.
I cry to you, O LORD;

I say, "You are my refuge,
  my portion in the land of the living. "   Psalm 142:4,5

"Be not far from me,
  for trouble is near,
  and there is none to help. "   Psalm 22:11

"Zion hears and is glad,
  and the daughters of Judah rejoice,
  because of your judgments, O LORD. "   Psalm 97:8

"Take hold of shield and buckler
  and rise for my help!"   Psalm 35:2

"Help us, O God of our salvation,
  for the glory of your name;
deliver us, and atone for our sins,
  for your name's sake!"   Psalm 79:9

✝**And let Soldiers, and all of us know, that if we obtain any victory over our enemies, it is our duty to give all the glory to the Lord, and say:**
  "The LORD is a man of war;
    the LORD is his name. "   Exodus 15:3

"Your right hand, O LORD, glorious in power,
  your right hand, O LORD, shatters the enemy.
In the greatness of your majesty you overthrow your adversaries;
  you send out your fury; it consumes them like stubble. " Exodus 15:6-7

"This is the LORD's doing;
  it is marvelous in our eyes. "   Psalm 118:23

"There has been no day like it before or since, when the LORD obeyed the voice of a man, for the LORD fought for Israel. "   Joshua 10:14

"But as for me, I will look to the LORD;
  I will wait for the God of my salvation;
  my God will hear me. "   Micah 7:7

"He delivered us from such a deadly peril, and he will deliver us. On him we have set our hope that he will deliver us again. "
                              2 Corinthians 1:10

"And now we thank you, our God, and praise your glorious name."
1 Chronicles 29:13

"And after all that has come upon us for our evil deeds and for our great guilt, seeing that you, our God, have punished us less than our iniquities deserved and have given us such a remnant as this, shall we break your commandments again and intermarry with the peoples who practice these abominations? Would you not be angry with us until you consumed us, so that there should be no remnant, nor any to escape?"
Ezra 9:13, 14

*"I have sworn an oath and confirmed it,
  to keep your righteous rules."*
Psalm 119:106

*"I will walk before the LORD
  in the land of the living."*
Psalm 116:9

FINIS

Appendix B

Of God, and of the Holy Trinity
(From the Westminster Confession of Faith)

I.   There is but one only,[1] living, and true God,[2] who is infinite in being and perfection,[3] a most pure spirit,[4] invisible,[5] without body, parts,[6] or passions;[7] immutable,[8] immense,[9] eternal,[10] incomprehensible,[11] almighty,[12]

---

[1] Deut. 6:4 "Hear, O Israel: The LORD our God, the LORD is one." 1Cor. 8:4,6 Therefore, as to the eating of food offered to idols, we know that "an idol has no real existence," and that "there is no God but one. yet for us there is one God, the Father, from whom are all things and for whom we exist, and one Lord, Jesus Christ, through whom are all things and through whom we exist."

[2] 1Thess. 1:9 "For they themselves report concerning us the kind of reception we had among you, and how you turned to God from idols to serve the living and true God." Jer. 10:10 But the LORD is the true God; he is the living God and the everlasting King. At his wrath the earth quakes, and the nations cannot endure his indignation."

[3] Job 11:7-9 "Can you find out the deep things of God? Can you find out the limit of the Almighty? It is higher than heaven—what can you do? Deeper than Sheol—what can you know? Its measure is longer than the earth and broader than the sea." Job 26:14 Behold, these are but the outskirts of his ways, and how small a whisper do we hear of him! But the thunder of his power who can understand?"

[4] John 4:24 "God is spirit, and those who worship him must worship in spirit and truth".

[5] 1Tim. 1:17 "To the King of ages, immortal, invisible, the only God, be honor and glory forever and ever. Amen."

[6] Deut. 4:15-16 "Therefore watch yourselves very carefully. Since you saw no form on the day that the LORD spoke to you at Horeb out of the midst of the fire, beware lest you act corruptly by making a carved image for yourselves, in the form of any figure, the likeness of male or female," John 4:24 "God is spirit, and those who worship him must worship in spirit and truth." Luke 24:39 "See my hands and my feet, that it is I myself. Touch me, and see. For a spirit does not have flesh and bones as you see that I have."

[7] Acts 14:11,15 "And when the crowds saw what Paul had done, they lifted up their voices, saying in Lycaonian, 'The gods have come down to us in the likeness of men!'" "Men, why are you doing these things? We also are men, of like nature with you, and we bring you good news, that you should turn from these vain things to a living God, who made the heaven and the earth and the sea and all that is in them."

[8] James 1:17 "Every good gift and every perfect gift is from above, coming down from the Father of lights with whom there is no variation or shadow due to change." Mal. 3:6 "For I the LORD do not change; therefore you, O children of Jacob, are not consumed."

most wise,[13] most holy,[14] most free,[15] most absolute;[16] working all things according to the counsel of His own immutable and most righteous will,[17] for His own glory;[18] most loving,[19] gracious, merciful, long-suffering, abundant in goodness and truth, forgiving iniquity, transgression, and sin;[20] the rewarder of them that diligently seek Him;[21] and withal, most just, and terrible in His judgments,[22] hating all sin,[23] and who will by no means clear the guilty.[24]

---

[9] 1 Kings 8:27 "But will God indeed dwell on the earth? Behold, heaven and the highest heaven cannot contain you; how much less this house that I have built!" Jer. 23:23,24 "Am I a God at hand, declares the LORD, and not a God afar off? Can a man hide himself in secret places so that I cannot see him? declares the LORD. Do I not fill heaven and earth? declares the LORD."

[10] Psa. 90:2 "Before the mountains were brought forth, or ever you had formed the earth and the world, from everlasting to everlasting you are God." 1Tim. 1:17 "To the King of ages, immortal, invisible, the only God, be honor and glory forever and ever. Amen."

[11] Psa. 145:3 "Great is the LORD, and greatly to be praised, and his greatness is unsearchable."

[12] Gen. 17:1 "When Abram was ninety-nine years old the LORD appeared to Abram and said to him, "I am God Almighty; walk before me, and be blameless." Rev. 4:8 "And the four living creatures, each of them with six wings, are full of eyes all around and within, and day and night they never cease to say, "Holy, holy, holy, is the Lord God Almighty, who was and is and is to come!"

[13] Rom. 16:27 "to the only wise God be glory forevermore through Jesus Christ! Amen."

[14] Isa. 6:3 "And one cried unto another, and said, Holy, holy, holy, is the Lord of hosts: the whole earth is full of his glory." Rev. 4:8 "And the four living creatures, each of them with six wings, are full of eyes all around and within, and day and night they never cease to say, "Holy, holy, holy, is the Lord God Almighty, who was and is and is to come!"."

[15] Psa. 115:3 "Our God is in the heavens; he does all that he pleases."

[16] Exodus 3:14 "God said to Moses, 'I AM WHO I AM.' And he said, 'Say this to the people of Israel, 'I AM has sent me to you.'"

[17] Eph. 1:11 In him we have obtained an inheritance, having been predestined according to the purpose of him who works all things according to the counsel of his will,

[18] Prov. 16:4 The LORD has made everything for its purpose, even the wicked for the day of trouble.

[19] 1John 4:8,16 Anyone who does not love does not know God, because God is love. So we have come to know and to believe the love that God has for us. God is love, and whoever abides in love abides in God, and God abides in him.

[20] Exodus 34:6 "The LORD passed before him and proclaimed, 'The LORD, the LORD, a God merciful and gracious, slow to anger, and abounding in steadfast love and faithfulness, 'keeping steadfast love for thousands, forgiving iniquity and transgression and sin, but who will by no means clear the guilty, visiting the iniquity of the fathers on the children and the children's children, to the third and the fourth generation.'"

[21] Heb. 11:6 And without faith it is impossible to please him, for whoever would draw near to God must believe that he exists and that he rewards those who seek him.

[22] Neh. 9:32,33 Now, therefore, our God, the great, the mighty, and the awesome God, who keeps covenant and steadfast love, let not all the hardship seem little to you that has come upon us, upon our kings, our princes, our priests, our prophets, our fathers, and all your people, since the time of the

II.   God has all life,[25] glory,[26] goodness,[27] blessedness,[28] in and of Himself; and is alone in and unto Himself all-sufficient, not standing in need of any creatures which He has made,[29] nor deriving any glory from them,[30] but only manifesting His own glory in, by, unto, and upon them. He is the alone fountain of all being, of whom, through whom, and to whom are all things;[31] and has most sovereign dominion over them, to do by them, for them, or upon them whatsoever Himself pleases.[32] In His sight all things are

---

kings of Assyria until this day. Yet you have been righteous in all that has come upon us, for you have dealt faithfully and we have acted wickedly.

[23] Psa. 5:5,6 The boastful shall not stand before your eyes; you hate all evildoers. You destroy those who speak lies; the LORD abhors the bloodthirsty and deceitful man.

[24] Nahum 1:2,3 The LORD is a jealous and avenging God; the LORD is avenging and wrathful; the LORD takes vengeance on his adversaries and keeps wrath for his enemies. The LORD is slow to anger and great in power, and the LORD will by no means clear the guilty. His way is in whirlwind and storm, and the clouds are the dust of his feet. Exodus 34:7, "keeping steadfast love for thousands, forgiving iniquity and transgression and sin, but who will by no means clear the guilty, visiting the iniquity of the fathers on the children and the children's children, to the third and the fourth generation."

[25] John 5:26 For as the Father has life in himself, so he has granted the Son also to have life in himself.

[26] Acts 7:2 "And Stephen said: 'Brothers and fathers, hear me. The God of glory appeared to our father Abraham when he was in Mesopotamia, before he lived in Haran,"

[27] Psa. 119:68 "You are good and do good; teach me your statutes."

[28] 1Tim. 6:15 which he will display at the proper time--he who is the blessed and only Sovereign, the King of kings and Lord of lords. Rom. 9:5 To them belong the patriarchs, and from their race, according to the flesh, is the Christ who is God over all, blessed forever. Amen."

[29] Acts 17:24,25 "The God who made the world and everything in it, being Lord of heaven and earth, does not live in temples made by man, nor is he served by human hands, as though he needed anything, since he himself gives to all mankind life and breath and everything."

[30] Job 22:2,3 "Can a man be profitable unto God, as he that is wise may be profitable unto himself? Is it any pleasure to the Almighty, that you are righteous? or is it gain to him that you make your ways perfect?"

[31] Rom. 11:36 "For from him and through him and to him are all things. To him be glory forever. Amen."

[32] Rev. 4:11 "Worthy are you, our Lord and God, to receive glory and honor and power, for you created all things, and by your will they existed and were created." 1Tim. 6:15 which he will display at the proper time—he who is the blessed and only Sovereign, the King of kings and Lord of lords." Dan. 4:25,35 "that you shall be driven from among men, and your dwelling shall be with the beasts of the field. You shall be made to eat grass like an ox, and you shall be wet with the dew of heaven, and seven periods of time shall pass over you, till you know that the Most High rules the kingdom of men and gives it to whom he will... all the inhabitants of the earth are accounted as nothing, and he does according to his will among the host of heaven and among the inhabitants of the earth; and none can stay his hand or say to him, "What have you done?"

open and manifest,[33] His knowledge is infinite, infallible, and independent upon the creature,[34] so as nothing is to Him contingent, or uncertain.[35] He is most holy in all His counsels, in all His works, and in all His commands.[36] To Him is due from angels and men, and every other creature, whatsoever worship, service, or obedience He is pleased to require of them.[37]

III.   In the unity of the Godhead there be three persons, of one substance, power, and eternity: God the Father, God the Son, and God the Holy Ghost:[38] the Father is of none, neither begotten, nor proceeding; the Son is eternally begotten of the Father;[39] the Holy Ghost eternally proceeding from the Father and the Son.[40]

---

[33] Heb. 4:13 "And no creature is hidden from his sight, but all are naked and exposed to the eyes of him to whom we must give account."

[34] Rom. 11:33,34 "Oh, the depth of the riches and wisdom and knowledge of God! How unsearchable are his judgments and how inscrutable his ways! "For who has known the mind of the Lord, or who has been his counselor?" Psa. 147:5 "Great is our Lord, and abundant in power; his understanding is beyond measure."

[35] Acts 15:18 Known unto God are all his works from the beginning of the world. Eze. 11:5 And the Spirit of the Lord fell upon me, and said unto me, Speak; Thus saith the Lord; Thus have ye said, O house of Israel: for I know the things that come into your mind, every one of them.

[36] Psa. 145:17 "The LORD is righteous in all his ways and kind in all his works." Rom. 7:12 "So the law is holy, and the commandment is holy and righteous and good."

[37] Rev. 5:12-14 "saying with a loud voice, "Worthy is the Lamb who was slain, to receive power and wealth and wisdom and might and honor and glory and blessing!" [13]And I heard every creature in heaven and on earth and under the earth and in the sea, and all that is in them, saying, "To him who sits on the throne and to the Lamb be blessing and honor and glory and might forever and ever!" [14]And the four living creatures said, "Amen!" and the elders fell down and worshiped."

[38] 1 John 5:7,8 "For there are three that testify: [8]the Spirit and the water and the blood; and these three agree." Matt. 3:16,17 "And when Jesus was baptized, immediately he went up from the water, and behold, the heavens were opened to him, and he saw the Spirit of God descending like a dove and coming to rest on him; [17]and behold, a voice from heaven said, "This is my beloved Son, with whom I am well pleased." 28:19 "Go therefore and make disciples of all nations, baptizing them in the name of the Father and of the Son and of the Holy Spirit" 2 Cor. 13:14 "The grace of the Lord Jesus Christ and the love of God and the fellowship of the Holy Spirit be with you all."

[39] John 1:14,15 "And the Word became flesh and dwelt among us, and we have seen his glory, glory as of the only Son from the Father, full of grace and truth. [15](John bore witness about him, and cried out, "This was he of whom I said, 'He who comes after me ranks before me, because he was before me.'")" 18 "No one has ever seen God; the only God, who is at the Father's side, he has made him known."

[40] John 15:26 "But when the Helper comes, whom I will send to you from the Father, the Spirit of truth, who proceeds from the Father, he will bear witness about me." Gal. 4:6 And because you are sons, God has sent the Spirit of his Son into our hearts, crying, "Abba! Father!"

APPENDIX C

PATRIOTIC ADDRESSES

My very dear Sarah,

The indications are very strong that we shall move in a few days-perhaps tomorrow. Lest I should not be able to write again, I feel impelled to write a few lines that may fall under your eye when I am no more.

I have no misgivings about, or lack of confidence in the cause in which I am engaged, and my courage does not halt or falter. I know how strongly American Civilization now leans on the triumph of the Government, and how great a debt we owe to those who went before us through the blood and suffering of the Revolution. And I am willing—perfectly willing—to lay down all the joys in this life, to help maintain this Government, and to pay that debt.

Sarah, my love for you is deathless. It seems to bind me with mighty cables that nothing but Omnipotence could break; and yet my love of country comes over me like a strong wind and bears me irresistibly on with all these chains to the battlefield.

The memories of the blissful moments I have spent with you come creeping over me, and I feel most grateful to God and to you that I have enjoyed them for so long. How hard it is for me to give them up and burn to ashes the hopes of future years, when, God willing, we might still have lived and loved together, and seen our sons grown up to honorable manhood around us. I have, I know, but few and small claims upon Divine Providence, but something whispers to me-perhaps it is the wafted prayer of my little Edgar, that I shall return to my loved ones unharmed. If I do not my dear Sarah, never forget how much I love you, and that when my last breath escapes me on the battlefield, it will whisper your name. Forgive my many faults, and the many pains I have caused you. How thoughtless and foolish I have often times been! How gladly would I wash out with my tears every little spot upon your happiness.

But, oh Sarah! If the dead can come back to this earth and flit unseen around those they loved, I shall always be near you; in the gladdest days and in the darkest nights...always, always. And if there be a soft breeze upon your cheek, it shall be my breath, and as the cool air fans your throbbing temple, it shall be my spirit passing by. Sarah, do not mourn me dead; think I am gone and wait for me, for we shall meet again.

Sullivan Ballou

(Sullivan Ballou was killed a week later at the battle of Bull Run)

"THE WAR IS ACTUALLY BEGUN"

Patrick Henry, March 23, 1775

"No man thinks more highly than I do of the patriotism, as well as abilities, of the very worthy gentlemen who have just addressed the house. But different men often see the same subject in different lights; and, therefore, I hope it will not be thought disrespectful to those gentlemen, if entertaining, as I do, opinions of a character very opposite to theirs, I shall speak forth my sentiments freely, and without reserve. This is no time for ceremony. The question before the house is one of awful moment to this country. For my own part, I consider it as nothing less than a question of freedom or slavery. And in proportion to the magnitude of the subject, ought to be the freedom of debate. It is only in this way that we can hope to arrive at truth and fulfill the great responsibility which we hold to God and our country. Should I keep back my opinions at such a time through fear of giving offense I should consider myself guilty of treason toward my country and of an act of disloyalty toward the majesty of Heaven which I revere above all earthly kings.

Mr. President it is natural for man to indulge in the illusions of hope. We are apt to shut our eyes against a painful truth—and listen to the song of the siren till she transforms us into beasts. Is this the part of wise men engaged in a great and arduous struggle for liberty? Are we disposed to be of the number of those who, having eyes, see not, and, having ears, hear not, the things which so nearly concern their temporal salvation? For my part, whatever anguish of spirit it might cost, I am willing to know the whole truth; to know the worst and provide for it.

I have but one lamp by which my feet are guided; and that is the lamp of experience. I know of no way of judging the future but by the past. And judging by the past, I wish to know what there has been in the conduct of the British ministry for the last ten years to justify those hopes with which gentlemen have been pleased to solace themselves and the house? Is it that insidious smile with which our petition has been lately received? Trust it not, sir; it will prove a snare to your feet. Suffer not yourselves to be betrayed with a kiss. Ask yourselves how this gracious reception of our petition comports with those war like preparations which cover our waters and darken our land. Are fleets and armies necessary to a work of love and reconciliation? Have we shown ourselves so unwilling to be reconciled that force must be called in to win back our love? Let us not deceive ourselves, sir. These are the implements of war and subjugation—the last arguments to which kings resort. I ask gentlemen, sir, what means this martial array if its purpose be not to force us to submission? Can gentlemen assign any other possible motive for it? Has Great Britain any enemy in this quarter of the world to call for all this accumulation of navies and armies? No, sir, she has none. They are meant for us: they can be meant for no other. They are sent over to bind and rivet upon us those chains which the British Ministry have been long forging. And what have we to oppose them? Shall we try argument? Sir, we have been trying that for the last ten years. Have we anything new to offer upon the subject? Nothing. We have held the subject up in every light of which it is capable; but it has been all in vain. Shall we resort to entreaty and humble supplication? What terms shall we find which have not been already exhausted? Let us not, I beseech you, sir, deceive ourselves longer. Sir, we have done everything that could be done to avert the storm which now coming on. We have petitioned—we have remonstrated—we have supplicated—we have prostrated ourselves before the throne, and have implored its interposition to arrest the tyrannical hands of the ministry and Parliament. Our petitions have been slighted; our remonstrances have produced additional violence and insult; our supplications have been disregarded; and we have been spurned, with contempt, from the foot of the throne. In vain, after these things, may we indulge the fond hope of peace and reconciliation. There is no longer any room for hope. If we wish to be free—if we mean to preserve inviolate those inestimable privileges for which we have been so long contending—if we mean not basely to abandon the noble struggle in which we have been so long engaged, and which we have pledged ourselves never to abandon until the glorious object of our contest shall be obtained—we must fight! I repeat it, sir, we must fight!! An appeal to arms and to the God of Hosts is all that is left us!

They tell us, sir, that we are weak—unable to cope with so formidable an adversary. But when shall we be stronger? Will it be the next week, or the next year? Will it be when we are totally disarmed, and when a British guard shall be stationed in every house? Shall we gather strength by irresolution and inaction? Shall we acquire the means of effectual resistance by lying supinely on our backs, and hugging the illusive phantom of Hope, until our enemies shall have bound us hand and foot? Sir, we are not weak, if we make a proper use of those means which the God of nature hath placed in our power. Three millions of people, armed in the holy cause of liberty, and in such a country as that which we posses are invincible by any force which our enemy can send against us. Besides, sir, we shall not fight our battles alone. There is a just God who presides over the destinies of nations, and who will raise up friends to fight our battles for us. The battle, sir, is not to the strong alone; it is to the vigilant, the active, the brave. Besides, sir, we have no election. If we were base enough to desire it, it is now too late to retire from the contest. There is no retreat, but in submission and slavery!

Our chains are forged; their clanking may be heard on the plains of Boston! The war is inevitable—and let it come!! I repeat it, sir, let it come!!!

It is in vain, sir, to extenuate the matter. Gentlemen may cry, peace, peace—but there is no peace. The war is actually begun. The next gale that sweeps from the North will bring to our ears the clash of resounding arms! Our brethren are already in the field! Why stand we here idle? What is it that gentlemen wish? What would they have? Is life so dear, or peace so sweet, as to be purchased at the price of chains and slavery? Forbid it, Almighty God! I know not what course others may take; but as for me, give me liberty or give me death!"

APPENDIX D

PARABLE OF THE BIG DOG

Imagine if you will, that a father hands his son the leash of a very large dog. The dog is not satisfied to walk at any leisurely pace but is constantly pulling at the leash as if it were in a hurry to get from one place to another (even though you know that dogs have no appointments to make or schedules to keep).

Now suppose that the father handed this leash of a powerful animal that was pulling ahead with all his force to his son, who was three years old. Barely able to walk, the boy soon is on his face being pulled across the ground by the dog who is neither hostile nor interested in the boys suffering. The dog only pushes ahead still determined to make it's goal. The boy for his part is unable to either stop the dog, or regain his feet. Left alone, he would certainly be dragged to his death.

The point of this parable is simple. Philosophers and psychologists have pointed out what the Scriptures have taught in other ways when they say that man is made of emotion, will, and reason. Some use the triad of the Id, the Ego, and the Super Ego. The first model is superior to this.

In the story of the dog, the dog will represent emotion, always pulling and powerful but untrained, undisciplined, and indifferent about the future welfare of the boy. The boy represents reason. Too young to be able to control the dog just as a child is born a slave to emotion and unable to reason what is best for the long term. As the child grows, that is as reason matures, he is able more and more to wrestle with emotion and rein it in, subjecting it to reason and ultimately to gain control of his will. This maturity requires a commitment to learning and a concerted effort to find and attain to wisdom. Proverbs promises,

"[1]My son, if you receive my words
and treasure up my commandments with you,
[2]making your ear attentive to wisdom
and inclining your heart to understanding;
[3]yes, if you call out for insight
and raise your voice for understanding,
[4]if you seek it like silver
and search for it as for hidden treasures,
[5]then you will understand the fear of the LORD
and find the knowledge of God.
[6]For the LORD gives wisdom;
from his mouth come knowledge and understanding;
[7]he stores up sound wisdom for the upright;
he is a shield to those who walk in integrity,
[8]guarding the paths of justice
and watching over the way of his saints.
[9]Then you will understand righteousness and justice
and equity, every good path;
[10]for wisdom will come into your heart,
and knowledge will be pleasant to your soul;
[11]discretion will watch over you,
understanding will guard you,
[12]delivering you from the way of evil,
from men of perverted speech,
[13]who forsake the paths of uprightness
to walk in the ways of darkness,
[14]who rejoice in doing evil
and delight in the perverseness of evil,
[15]men whose paths are crooked,
and who are devious in their ways."
(Proverbs 2:1-15)

ENDNOTES

[1] http://www.wsu.edu/~dee/REFORM/ZWINGLI.HTM

[2] http://www.ccel.org/s/schaff/hcc8/htm/iv.v.vi.htm

[3] The Soldier's Creed

[4] ibid

[5] Commentary on the Old Testament, (Hendrickson Publishers, Inc., Peabody, Massachusetts,1996) p. 923

[6] The manifestation of the kingdom of darkness, or of evil in any age. The opposite of righteousness and the Kingdom of God.

[7] Andre Comte-Sponville, *A Small Treatise on the Great Virtues*, Henry holt and Company, 2001, p. 140

[8] William G. T. Shedd, *Dogmatic Theology*, Presbyterian and Reformed Publishing Company, 2003, p. 804.

[9] Andre Comte-Sponville, *A Small Treatise on the Great Virtues*, Henry Holt and Company, 2001, p. 52

[10] An excerpt from *"An Introduction to St. Paul's Letter to the Romans,"* Luther's German Bible of 1522, by Martin Luther, 1483-1546

[11] *Corporal Horatio D. Chapman, Company C, 20th Connecticut Volunteers, Civil War Diary of a Forty-niner, pages 22-24.*

[12] Matthew Henry, Commentary on Job 5

[13] Matthew Henry, Commentary on Matthew 18

[14] Christopher Lasch, *The Culture of Narcissism, American Life in An Age of Diminishing Expectations*, W.W.Norton & Company, 1991, p.72-73.

[15] The Soldiers Pocket Bible was a short tract originally published for the Parliamentary Army during the English Civil War, 1643. It was a small 16 page publication made to fit literally in the soldier's pocket. It is revised and updated here for the American Military.

Printed in the United States
104927LV00005B/64-111/A